How to Bring God's Super to Your Natural

Agreeing with God and Releasing His Kingdom

DICK HOCHREITER

How to Bring God's Super to Your Natural:
Agreeing with God & Releasing His Kingdom
by Dick Hochreiter

Copyright © 2006, 2009, 2012 Dick Hochreiter

ISBN: 978-0-9824971-0-4

Contact Dick at www.theprayercompany.com
or at dick@theprayercompany.com.

See www.theprayercompany.com for the brochure "God's Real Bailout,"
and Armed and Dangerous 7+7 Anointing Oil at wholesale pricing.

To subscribe to "My Daily Dose," see the Links page
on www.theprayercompany.com.

Printed in the United States of America

Endorsements

"As Dick's friend and former pastor, I have learned a lot from him. This book has challenged me to think differently about helping people to be kingdom minded, instead of getting stuck inside the four walls of the church building. I highly recommend this book to any pastor who wants to encourage his or her congregation to 'go into all the world' to make kingdom disciples."

MARC STAMPER
Bloomington Christian School
Bloomington, CA

"I've known Dick for over forty-five years. He was a fighter growing up, but now he fights the good fight of faith. I've been a part of many of his stories and have had the pleasure to advance the kingdom of God with Dick all over the world. What you will read in this book is real life, and the principles really work."

LARRY IHLE
Dexterity Dental Arts
Farmington, MN

"As a pastor, I am so excited about Dick's book. It is really helping the players of "Team Jesus" to find their way out of the locker room and into the harvest field. It is a must-read for every member of the body of Christ."

STEVE BRAUN
Banning Foursquare Church
Banning, California

"Dick Hochreiter, my father-in-law, has always modeled for me what it means to be a doer of the Word and not just a hearer. He experiences what so many believers only talk about. Whether it is visiting with him in his home, or assisting him on one of his many ventures, I always walk away challenged to live out my faith and encouraged to help my congregation to the same."

CHRIS FRALEY
Wildwood Calvary Chapel
Yucaipa, California

Acknowledgements

SPECIAL THANKS to...my wife Carol and my loving family. Larry & Rose Ihle; Bruce & Sue Nelson; Ken & Carrie Beaudry; Joe and Amy Senser; Dennis Potter; Randy Cleary. George Otis, Jr., and Graham Powers. Ed Silvoso and the Harvest Evangelism team. Pastor Kip and Marlys Jentoft. Aleks & Violeta from Albania; Melissa Logan; David Culbertson; Pastors Steve & Liz Braun and team; Pastors Chris Fraley, Scott Wright and team; Pastors Marc & Brenda Stamper; Jonathan & Jessica and Derrick Mathe and youth; Mike Landingham and team; Brandon Cernoch and Kelly Claussen from Stout University. The kingdom coaches and disciples in the Pass Area: Marc Stamper, Shane Nerenberg, Dan Crayne, Jim Scantlin, Carlos Lamas, Bob Wilerson, Rick Lance, Sharon Fish, Steve and Liz Braun, John Ayres, Dr. Bola Arowolo, Jerry Westholder, Bobby and Tina Childs, Gabriel Ward, Brian Vanderbyl. All the unemployed workers that have gone out with us (and those who have now found jobs). Josh Wiedrick: I thank God for our friendship and look forward to being with you in God's presence again. We love you! David Sluka for his partnership in the writing and publication of this book. John Hanka for the cover design.

Contents

The bad news is that you were born under a curse. The good news is that Jesus has broken that curse so that you can experience freedom. Jesus wants to release creativity and power through you each day to advance His kingdom to those still under the curse.

God is speaking today and you can hear His voice. Those who know God's voice know His heart and will see His will done on earth as it is in heaven.

Prophetic acts are the actions that come when you listen and respond to God's voice. These acts produce kingdom power with kingdom results.

Advancing God's kingdom is a full-contact sport. When two kingdoms collide, there will be a clash and a whole lot of dust.

Jesus changed the lives of those He encountered. Living the kingdom way always leaves your world different than you found it.

Jesus came to destroy the works of the enemy. Since God made you to be Christ-like, He expects you to do the same as you walk in His character and power.

Foreword
by Steve Braun

WHAT AN INCREDIBLE PRIVILEGE it is for me to introduce you to Dick Hochreiter. He is one of the greatest guys I know. Dick's incredible love for others is only surpassed by his deep love for our Lord. When I first met Dick ten years ago, I asked him, "So what do you do for a living?" And he replied, "Oh, just bust nations open for Jesus." He wasn't kidding!

There's a scripture in the Bible that Dick has quoted to me many times. It is Matthew 24:14 and it says, "And this gospel of the kingdom will be preached in the whole world as a testimony to all nations, and then the end will come." If Dick were the only Christian in the world, he would attempt to accomplish this assignment by himself. Fortunately, he's not the only one, but it's my prayer that this book will inspire you to jump in and help.

Dick often uses analogies from the game of football to teach and inspire others. One of my favorites is of the body of Christ sitting in the grand stands cheering the full time ministers on as they do ministry. Dick cries out to the Lord, "Put 'em in coach!"

The days ahead will be intense, but they will also be the greatest opportunities for ministry ever. Surely the Lord will raise up everyone in the body of Christ who is willing to help Him with this last days' harvest. As you read this book, take the time to ask the Lord how you too can come out of the locker room and take part in bringing God's kingdom to earth!

STEVE BRAUN
Pastor, Banning Foursquare Church
Banning, California

God's 30-Day Curse Back Guarantee

The bad news is that you were born under a curse. The good news is that Jesus has broken that curse so that you can experience freedom. Jesus wants to release creativity and power through you each day to advance His kingdom to those still under the curse.

Have you ever wondered why life can be so good, and why life can be so bad? From the beginning of time, God loved you and had a very good plan for your life. He made you to be creative. God made you to be a blessing wherever you go and speak life into every situation you are in. The Bible says that Jesus Christ came to give life—

How to Bring God's Super to Your Natural

life more abundant than what you've known (John 10:10).
The purpose of the *good* in your life is to draw you to God
(Romans 2:4).

You are in a war zone

A war began long ago between God and a rebellious
angel who wanted to be like God. Lucifer, this angel turned
devil, got kicked out of heaven. Out of his hatred for God, he
has been trying to get back at Him ever since. The battle you
face in life is Satan's effort to hurt God by perverting God's
original intent for your life. This is why life can be so *bad*.

The devil comes to steal God's plan

The devil has a hell of a plan for your life. Jesus Christ
called the devil a thief who comes to steal, kill, and destroy.
The thief wants to steal your family. He tries to put so much
stress on you at work it kills you.

If you do not understand that there is an enemy who
is out to destroy what God wants to do in you, you are not
equipped for the battle that rages daily over your life.

God has a special deal for you today

While in Argentina a number of years ago, some friends
and I went to visit a family that owned a business. They
had a religious understanding of God and the Bible, but
did not have any real relationship with the Lord. The guy
who brought us to the home warned us, "Be careful, these
folks are good friends of mine and I don't want to hurt
our relationship."

So we prayed for God's wisdom and the Lord showed us how to help this family. We followed Jesus' example from Luke 10:1-9 to speak peace to them, fellowship with them, pray for the needs they had, and share that the kingdom of God had come near to them.

It started with Adam and Eve

We were welcomed by the mom, her two adult sons, and the maid. After we sat down and got to know them a bit, the Lord showed me that I was to speak about His original intent in the Garden of Eden—that He created Adam and Eve and placed them in the Garden to have a close relationship with them and with those who would come after them.

Sin brought a curse into a world of blessing

But Adam and Eve disobeyed God by eating the fruit of the tree of the knowledge of good and evil. When they ate, their disobedience released sin and death into the world, and God had to drive Adam and Eve out of the Garden.

God had a plan to break the curse

The Bible says that before the foundation of the world, God had a plan to send His Son (Hebrews 4:3, also chapters 8-10). He didn't take the neighbor kid; He took His own Son because redeeming the world He had made was so important to Him. God wanted to have an intimate friendship with us and had a plan to bring things back to order again.

Jesus came on the scene to break the curse

About two thousand years ago, God's Son took the form of baby Jesus. He was sent to live on earth as Messiah (the Christ) to show us what God the Father was like and then die on a cross to break the curse that came into the world through sin (1 John 14:7-11, 1 John 3:8).

The Lord showed me that I needed to tell this family that unless they were under the covering of the blood of Jesus that was shed at the cross; the curse was still on each of them, their business, and their home.

Faith in Jesus, not our works, breaks the curse

The judgment against sin is the death penalty (Genesis 3:1-19; Romans 6:23). Since Adam and Eve, all humanity has failed to live according to God's laws and is also under the death penalty (Romans 3:19-28). God's plan was that a spotless sacrifice die in place of the guilty and become a curse so they could receive God's blessings. Jesus perfectly obeyed God's law, became that substitute, and redeemed us from the curse.

51 percent good and 49 percent bad doesn't cut it

The world thinks that if you do more good than bad you're ok with God. But good deeds can never reverse the curse and make anyone right with God. The Bible says that all who try to live by good works are under the curse and are headed for destruction (Galatians 3:10-11). Even if you did good 99.9 percent of the time, the Bible says that in

God's eyes your goodness is worth as much as a filthy rag (Isaiah 64:6-7). Also that .1 percent bad still earns you the death sentence.

Only through faith in Christ's work, not our own, can we come out from under the curse and not have to live and die separated from God (Galatians 2:16-3:26). Those who put their trust in Christ can be blessed, receive God's favor, and have fellowship with God.

This family had a choice to stay under the curse or come out through Jesus—the only way God the Father has provided to come out from darkness into God's light (John 5:24; John 14:5-7).

You have to come out from under the curse

I said "This was God's plan for you from the beginning—to break the curse off of you—but right now your business and all parts of your lives are still under the curse." I continued, "It's your choice. You can stay under the curse or you can come out and have the power of God in your lives. It doesn't mean that there won't be problems, but God will help you in your business and He'll do things to encourage you in every part of your lives. If you'd like that, we can help you because that's why the Lord brought us here. So what do you think?"

The woman and one of her sons responded. "Well, who wouldn't want to come out from under the curse? We need all the help we can get in our business." But the other son just looked at me. I thought, He's hearing what I'm saying but he's really not getting it.

God's 30-day curse back guarantee

So I said to him, "Since you are a business person, I believe that the Lord has a special deal for you today. He's going to give you a 30-day curse back guarantee. If you come out from under the curse and don't like it within thirty days, you can have all your curses back. Whatever you want to do is up to you, but this is business, God's business. So what do you think? He started to laugh and said, "I need all the help I can get from God. Why wouldn't I try that?" Then the maid said, "I want to come out too!"

Guarantee 1: Salvation from the curse. So we led all of them in a prayer to receive the Lord. They thanked Christ for forgiving their sins, for breaking the curse off their lives and their business, and for setting them free to be who God made them to be (Galatians 5).

Guarantee #2: Deliverance. These people knew they had been putting their trust in other places besides God. We said, "We all need to be delivered from the things that want to set up their kingdoms in our lives. God has given us authority to drive out the evil in our lives through the name of Jesus Christ by his shed blood."

We prayed that all of the things that had taken the place of God in the past—all the little gods they had worshiped and put before God—would be put under the feet of Jesus (Ephesians 1:22).

Guarantee 3: The three works of the Holy Spirit. It is no good to sweep a house clean and not fill it with the proper things. We said, "Now the Holy Spirit wants to come in and fill you where this stuff has left. Let's pray so you can be filled with the Holy Spirit."

There are three works of the Holy Spirit. First, the conviction of the Holy Spirit showed this family and the maid that they were under the curse and lost without Christ (1 John 16:8).

Second, they experienced the regeneration or the re-birth of their spirits by the Spirit of God coming into their lives when they prayed to receive Christ (John 20:22).

But to have the full package, they also needed to ask the Holy Spirit to come upon them (Acts 1:8). Some Christians argue that they have the Holy Spirit, which is true. The Holy Spirit is in them. However, they also need the Holy Spirit to come upon them with His power—power to be witnesses.

So we prayed that the Holy Spirit would both fill these four and come upon them with His power to be witnesses. After we prayed, the joy of the Lord was upon them.

Guarantee #4: Creativity and blessing. We said to the mother and her sons, "If it's ok with you, let's go to your plant to speak blessings over your business and release God's blessing and anointing over you. God wants to release the creativity He has intended for you to work in all of your life."

We went to the company and prayed for God's release of creativeness and anointing for business. As a part of God's kingdom and with the authority God had given them over their employees, we told them their mission was to help bring people and their work out from under the curse. We also prayed for their workers.

This family was so excited. They knew they had been delivered and God was going to help them. I saw hope in their eyes that was not present when we first entered their home.

God's Kingdom comes when invited

This family welcomed the kingdom of God as it drew near to them. They understood that the primary purpose of the Body of Christ is to redeem souls and the land from the curse, and to bring the kingdom of God to the marketplace. When a business does this, God's kingdom flows, that business is a blessing instead of a curse, and others can receive from that blessing.

People avoid God because they do not know His heart. Even after our initial salvation into God's family, we can find ourselves missing many of God's blessings because we buy into the lies of the enemy.

God's heart for the lost is freedom

One portion of Scripture that ministers to me is Luke 4:18, which is quoting from Isaiah 61. We can see the heart of God and why He sent Jesus: to bring good news to the afflicted, to heal the brokenhearted, to proclaim liberty to the captives and freedom to the prisoners, to comfort those who mourn. This heart of God was expressed through Jesus' ministry.

God also wants this heart of Jesus to be expressed through His Church. We can offer freedom to the bound. We can give sight to blind—physical and spiritual. The Bible says that Satan has blinded the minds of unbelievers so they cannot see the light of the gospel of Christ (2 Corinthians 4:3-4).

When I pray for people, I often pray that anything hindering them from seeing how much God loves them would be removed in the name of Jesus Christ. This breaks and removes the blinding spirit from their eyes. Then they have a fair chance to know God and feel His heart for them, whereas before they could not see clearly, if at all.

God wants to bless everyone

Do you believe God wants to bless everyone? I find that most people believe that God only wants to bless some; He doesn't want to bless everyone.

Recently I was a few seats away from a woman on an airplane who was visibly sick. I felt God wanted me to pray for her. I said to the woman sitting next to her, "I'm a minister and I'd love to pray for that woman if she wants me too. Could you ask her?" She asked and the lady said, "Yes, of course. Please!" She had a migraine that wasn't going away. I switched seats so I could sit next to the lady with the migraine, anointed her with oil, and prayed for her.

A woman sitting on the other side of the woman I was praying for said to me, "Do you do this often?" I replied, "Just when the Lord shows me that people need help. I like to help them." She asked me if I was a minister. "Well, I responded, "Not like you would understand. I minister in the marketplace around the world."

She then inquired what I do when I go into businesses. I told her we pray and bless. "These are all believers, right?" she asked. "No, not necessarily. We just go wherever God leads us. We minister to believers or unbelievers. That doesn't matter to us."

A religious spirit is exclusive

This woman's attitude changed immediately. She said "You can't just bless people." Without using the exact words, she basically went on to explain. "God doesn't want to bless everyone, only certain people."

I must admit that what she was communicating fired me up and I said as gently as I could, "If God didn't want to bless everyone; Jesus would have jumped off the cross and kicked the tails of those who were crucifying Him. But He chose to say, 'Father forgive them.' And He wasn't forgiving just a select few."

Then the woman I had prayed for opened her eyes and said, "That's right, I feel much better now. Thank God you prayed for me."

There is a religious spirit out there that says God doesn't want to bless everyone. If you've believed this, you've bought into a lie. This lie will destroy not only the blessings in your own life, but will also keep you from blessing those God wants you to bless. I find that many professing Christians don't believe Jesus died to break the curse off everyone. But this blessing and every other blessing is for the whole world, not just for certain folks.

That's why the Holy Spirit spoke to me to pray for this woman. When I responded to His heart, she was freed from her migraine.

God wants relationship not religion

A religious spirit would never want to bless a person in sin. In fact, this same religious spirit killed Jesus, Stephen, Peter, Paul, and other followers of Christ throughout church history in an attempt to stop the Good News of the Gospel.

But Christ's Spirit, at the moment of greatest weakness, forgave and blessed. The Bible clearly shows us God sent his Son to save the world, not condemn it (1 John 3:16-21) so we must kick out the spirit that wants to judge and condemn, and bless and speak life instead. God's heart is to give life, not to take life.

The Lord doesn't want your religious practices. He wants to have a relationship with you. This relationship means loving Him and loving others by esteeming them higher than ourselves. As Christ's body on earth, we are to demonstrate His heart to bless others.

By the way; the woman who gave me the hard time about blessing everyone did have a change of heart. As we were getting off the airplane she said, "Now I see how blessing people works. Thank you for praying for the lady. I need to do that more."

I'd like to pray for you right now: *In Jesus' name, I bind every religious spirit that has hindered you from the relationship God has intended for you to have with Him.*

Come out from under the curse

Freedom from the curse doesn't just happen, it must be *received*. If you have not come out from under the curse through faith in Jesus Christ, the Bible says that you are still living under the curse. The best you can hope for in this condition is some self-generated comfort for a few years on earth. Unfortunately, you cannot avoid the eternal hell that awaits those who remain under the curse. Maybe today your life is a living hell and what I'm sharing is good news to you.

This is the Good News: God the Father provided His Son, Jesus, to pay the penalty for your sins by shedding His blood on the cross. It's up to you if you want to stay under the curse or come out. Here are a few simple steps you can take right now.

Step 1: Come out from under the curse. Pray the following or something like it in your own words. *"Lord, forgive me for my sin—for all the things I thought were important, but actually just led me away from you. I receive your forgiveness through the power of your blood that was shed for me on the cross. Thank you for your love and mercy and that you made a way for me to come into your presence through your son Jesus. Thank you for breaking the curse off me, my job (or business), and my life."*

As God brings to mind sins or things you have put in front of God, ask God to forgive each thing. When you're done, thank Him for His work.

Step 2: Break the power of the curse. Pray, *"With the authority you've given to me as a child of God, I break off everything that has tried to keep me from being who you've called me to be. I renounce those spirits and the fear of man in the name of Jesus Christ."*

As you see things that have separated you from the love of God, renounce those things. *"I break the power of these acts of disobedience and I renounce the sin of ____. I command all this evil to go under the feet of Jesus Christ."* Each day break every curse and command it to go under the feet of Jesus Christ.

Step 3: Ask the Holy Spirit, *"Fill every vacancy where these other things have filled my life. Fill every part of me to overflowing with the living essence of your Spirit. I ask that your living waters would flow daily from my innermost being."* Each day you can pray, *"Today, help me to be a river of life and a river of blessing to those who are hurting in this world."*

Step 4: Release of creativity and anointing.

"I pray that the things you have had planned for my life from the foundation of time would be released right now and in the days ahead." Each day you can pray, *"God, loose the creativity and anointing that you want me to walk in today. Help me to see things the way you see them, hear the way you hear, and speak the way you speak."*

The acts continue through you

The gospels in the Bible (Matthew, Mark, Luke, and John) speak of the acts of Jesus—how Jesus ministered in his fleshly body as He was here on earth. After Jesus was crucified on the cross and ascended into heaven, Jesus started a new ministry through His new body, the Church. The book of Acts follows the work of the Holy Spirit as Christ was working through His Church.

We are Christ's body working on earth in this day and age. In a way, the book of Acts is still being written today through His Church, through our lives.

But we must be Holy Spirit led, just as Christ's first followers were. The Word of God is a playing field that shows us the boundaries, and we get to play within these boundaries. The Bible is also the playbook from which the Holy Spirit calls the plays. We must listen closely to the Coach to hear the plays He calls and execute what He says, which we'll be looking at in the next chapter.

God promises to be with you

God doesn't bring us into His family and then leave us to ourselves. The Bible tells us that God will complete what He begins (Philippians 1:6). If you have come out from under the curse, that is just the beginning of your walk with Christ.

I doubt you'll take the curse back guarantee after thirty days. I must warn you, however, that the war still rages, pain and tragedy still are a part of this life. But now you're on the winning side. You're getting your orders from the Holy Spirit, which will lead you into the blessings of God and eternal life.

Take Action

- Buy a Bible if you don't already have one. Start reading in *Genesis* (how it all began), *Mark* (the life of Jesus), and *Acts* (the life of the early Church).

- Come out from under the curse. If you have not, repent of your sins (turn away from them), ask Christ to forgive you and break the curse off every area in your life. (See John 3:1-21; Acts 2:37-39; 1 John 1:8-10.)

- Pursue a genuine relationship with God, not only religious activities. (See Mark 12:30-31.)

- Allow Jesus' heart to be expressed through you. Bless everyone, even those you think do not deserve it. (See Luke 6:27-28.)

God's Super to Your Natural

God is speaking today and you can hear His voice.
Those who know God's voice know His heart and
will see His will done on earth as it is in heaven.

If you have a boss and you're a productive worker, you do what your boss tells you to do. You know that it is important to listen when your boss gives you instructions to help you do your job better. When you listen and do what you're told, your boss is pleased with you, you are more productive, good things happen, and you keep getting a paycheck!

If you understand this, then you know how to bring the super to the natural: by hearing and following the Boss's orders. That Boss is God.

Bringing God's supernatural power into the marketplace takes more than just a good idea or natural man-made strategies. It takes hearing the voice of God. The issue is if we want to listen.

You can hear God's voice

The Bible says that the legalistic traditions of man have nullified the word of God, or may I say the *voice* of God (Matthew 15:1-9). Satan and his demonic spirits lie about God and how He wants to communicate with those He created. For example, when I share with others that God speaks to me, I get comments like "*You* hear from *God?*" "You think you hear God's *voice?*"

We *can* hear God. If we don't hear God's voice, we need to tune up our relationship with Him. God wants to have a daily conversation with us. He wants us to wake up in the morning and say, "Good morning, Lord. What's on the agenda for today?"

Hearing and acting brings breakthrough

Recently a friend asked me to talk to his dad who was dying of cancer. His dad had one arm amputated in the war and is a former defense attorney. My friend said, "I want to take you to see my dad because you're an ex-marine and maybe you can talk to him about the Lord. I don't think he's a believer." So we went.

I remember telling the dad that Jesus was a defense attorney so he was in good company defending the defenseless. But he wouldn't receive any of my encouragement about how much God cared for him. I left feeling very sad. I thought, "Wow, this guy is so hard. He doesn't even want to know God. I guess some people are just going to hell."

Some time later my friend called again. I was willing to go, but only for him. I didn't think I could help his dad, but I knew that people had been praying for him. As I was driving to see him, the Lord spoke to me a surprising word: "This man knows me. He knows my voice." Then God showed me that he had been wounded by a religious spirit (a demonic spirit). His hardness was toward religion and not the Lord.

When I walked into his room I saw a Bible sitting beside his bed. It was like the Lord saying. "See?" I sat down with him and made small talk. Then I said, "I see you read your Bible. Do you study it?" He replied, "Yeah, sometimes I do." I continued, "The Lord showed me this morning that you know Him." As I looked into his eyes, he started tearing up. I said, "The Lord also showed me that you have been wounded by a religious spirit. But God loves you and cares for you very much." He looked at me and said, "You're the first born-again Christian who has told me that I know God. I've only had people tell me how awful I am and that I'm going to hell."

Hearing the voice of God was the only way to penetrate what we were up against with that man. As unlikely as it seemed, I discovered that this man and God had a relationship. God just wanted me to encourage him at a time of great discouragement.

God's voice reflects God's heart of blessing

The Lord initially taught me to hear His voice by showing me Galatians 5:16-22. These Bible verses tell followers of Christ to walk in the *Spirit* and not in the *flesh*. The Bible says that the flesh and the Spirit constantly oppose each other so that you do not do the things you should.

The voice of the flesh curses

The Bible says that the voice or desire of the flesh is sexual immorality, impure thoughts and lustful deeds; idolatry and witchcraft; hatred, discord, jealousy, outbursts of anger, selfish ambition, dissensions, divisions, and envy; drunkenness, wild parties, and other kinds of sin. The Bible explains that no one who practices these things will inherit the kingdom of God.

The voice of the Spirit blesses

The voice or the fruit of the Spirit is love, joy, peace, patience, kindness, goodness, faithfulness, gentleness and self-control. When you walk by the Spirit, you will not carry out the desires of the flesh.

When I would hear things that were contrary to the Spirit, I knew it was not God speaking to me. When I would hear things of love, joy, peace, patience, kindness, goodness, faithfulness, gentleness and self-control, I knew it was the heart or voice of God.

Hindrances keep us from hearing God's voice

Many years ago, the extent of my Christianity was listening to a preacher, not hearing God for myself. I remember going home from church and talking about how well the preacher did that day. It seemed like my whole week was determined by *his* performance.

I used to think, "When do I get to do something?" I knew I wasn't a Sunday school teacher. My first try was disastrous. Others were always better at what there was to do inside the church building.

I felt different at work. I remember thinking, "I really can't mess up too bad because nobody here knows God. They're cursing and swearing all day long. I guess I can't send them to hell twice. It can only help if I talk to them a little bit about God."

But I was afraid of hearing God's voice. Also, I had been taught that God doesn't talk to people today like He did in the Bible. If for some reason God *would* speak today, I didn't think He would want to talk to me. These things made it difficult to want to hear from God, even though the things I was hearing in my spirit were the things that I wanted to do for God.

Is God confused or am I?

On my first trip to Mongolia, the Lord spoke to me about praying for a man in a wheelchair. I had never prayed for the sick before. At the time I was so unfamiliar with the voice of the Lord, I didn't know if it was the voice of God or the devil trying to set me up. I was very confused about what God wanted. I knew God loved this man, and I knew that Jesus healed many people in the Bible.

However, I had never seen God heal anyone so I didn't know if that was something He wanted to do today. Maybe the guy was crippled just because he was crippled and God wanted it that way.

I remember telling the Lord on the plane ride home, "I don't ever want to go to that nation again. I have nothing to offer." I wondered if God was double minded, or maybe I was the one confused. Maybe I didn't hear from God about the guy in the wheelchair.

The enemy had lied to me, saying, "There's no way you can reach these people. It is impossible." Amidst my own confusion, I knew God cared for those people and he wanted me to do something about it.

God does speak to us

The first time I really believed God wanted to speak to me was at a Wednesday night church meeting. The pastor looked at me at the end of his teaching and said, "God has given me a word for you." No one had ever said this to me.

He said, "The next time the Lord asks you to pray for the sick, you need to do it."

As the pastor spoke to me, I knew that God was alive and well and I had heard His voice. I thought, "God really does speak to me!"

In fact, God had been speaking to me all along, even about the crippled guy. At a time when Mongolia was the hardest country in the world to reach, I returned eight more times and helped to start the first church in the country, all by hearing God's voice and obeying.

After the pastor's word to me, I began to recognize God's voice saying, "Bless that person," or "Pray for that person." I would think, "Okay, how do I do that? What should I do next knowing that it is God who is asking me to do this?" Obedience became simpler as I realized I was not hearing my heart, but God's heart for that person. God's heart is far more tender for people than our own.

God wants to bless others through you

The Lord showed me I shouldn't go and say, "I want to pray for you," or "I want to bless you." I was to say, "The Lord has spoken to me and He wants to bless you." Or "God wants me to pray for you. Is that okay?" Many people will simply receive because they already know they need prayer. The Holy Spirit is already working on them. We only need to respond to what God wants us to do to express *His* heart.

God wants us to partner with Him in His plan

In the marketplace and every place we go each day, I believe God is speaking to us. God wants to free us so we can get past ourselves and allow Him to work through us. This is what He has intended from the time Jesus ascended to the Father and sent the Holy Spirit to the Church.

The Head wants to use His body

God wants to move through us all the time because we're His body. Imagine your head telling your body to do something and your body refusing to respond.

Many followers of Christ have been in this situation for a long time in their faith. God says something and His church body doesn't hear the message, ignores it, or dismisses it completely. The Head—*Christ*—wants His body—*us*—to listen and respond to His voice.

Obedience—not guilt—is fruitful

A religious spirit will try to get you to do things out of guilt. However, the Holy Spirit is a Spirit of liberty who says, "I have a work for you and it's not burdensome. You are free to do *what* God tells you to do, *when* and *how* the Lord tells you to do it."

I knew God wanted me to bless people, pray for people, and encourage people, so I used to feel bad about not talking to some people about Him. I don't anymore. I haven't experienced good results when I have tried to do something out of guilt. However, as I listen to the voice of God and pray for the people He leads me to, I see the power of God.

Jesus walked from place to place and didn't minister to everyone. But Jesus' obedience to the Father affected all of creation. God is really good at making sure no one gets left out. He *will* send help to those in need. That help may or may not be you. The key is to listen to what the Spirit of the Lord is telling *you*.

God wants us to listen to Him and to do what He wants to do. That's why our obedience is so important and so powerful. Our obedience brings *God's* super into our natural to impact the people *He* loves. Obedience to the Spirit of the Lord is what produces fruit in the kingdom of God.

God ideas work better than good ideas

If you want to be successful wherever you go and move God's kingdom forward, find out what God's heart is in the matter. We've got a lot of good ideas, but we need to *hear* what God wants and *act* upon it.

Next, let's look to the Bible to see how people heard from God and what they did about it.

Take Action

- Realize that you can and *need* to hear God's voice. Your life depends on it. (See John 10:1-5.)
- Seek God through prayer and reading the Bible. (See 2 Timothy 2:15.)
- Ask God to speak to you and believe He will. (See John 10:27-29.)

Prophetic Acts

*Prophetic acts are the actions that come when
you listen and respond to God's voice. These acts
produce kingdom power with kingdom results.*

In the Bible and in the world today we can see God's supernatural power come to the natural through *prophetic* acts. What is a prophetic act? In the Bible, a *prophet* was someone who heard from God and spoke to the people what God had said. A *prophetic act* is *hearing* from God and *acting* on what God has said.

Examples of prophetic acts

One Sunday I went with a friend to speak in Albert Lea, Minnesota. On our way to the church, the Lord spoke to me about prophetic acts. He said, "I'm going to make you a professor, professing prophetic acts. I want you to teach on it this morning in the service." I thought, *It would be helpful if I knew what a prophetic act was!* I said to the Lord, "You show me what to do and I'll do it."

During the service, the Lord directed me to share the following examples from the Bible.

Naaman is healed of leprosy

"Second Kings 5 tells the story of Naaman, a valiant warrior and captain of the army of Aram. But he also had leprosy. A Jewish servant girl told Naaman's wife about Elisha, a prophet in Israel. Naaman went to visit Elisha. Elisha told him to go to the muddy Jordan River and dunk himself seven times.

Naaman was initially upset at Elisha's instructions, but he eventually did what he was told. He acted on the word from the prophet and he was healed." I said, "That's a prophetic act. He *heard* the prophet, and he *acted*."

Joshua defeats a city

I continued, "Let's go to Joshua and the battle of Jericho found in Joshua 6. God told them to march around the city once each day for six days. On the seventh day, they were to march around the city seven times, blow the trumpets, and shout really loud. God told Joshua that when they did, the walls of the city would go flat.

"When the Israelites were walking around the walls, the people inside were probably thinking, 'Them folks are real stupid. What are they doing walking around like that thinking something's gonna happen.' But when Joshua and the people obeyed God, everyone knew the power of God had shown up. Joshua *listened* to God and *obeyed*. That's a prophetic act."

Jesus heals a blind man

"John 9 records that one day a blind man came to Jesus. Jesus spit in the dirt, made some clay, put it on his eyes, and told him to go wash in a pool. You would think that Jesus should have done something more accepted by the medical community of the day. But Jesus *heard* the voice of His Father and *acted*. The man obeyed Jesus and was healed."

Hear God's voice and act

I explained, "These are all prophetic acts. Naaman heard the voice of the prophet and acted. Joshua heard the Lord's voice and acted. John 5:19 records that Jesus only did what He heard the Father tell him to do. When He did, the power of God showed up.

"In each of these examples, it was God's heart to do it the way it was done, no matter how foolish it appeared at the time."

Our weakness + obedience = Kingdom power

The Lord then showed me prophetic acts in my own life. When my company was buried in debt and I had no way to get out, He spoke to me to repent of debt. I repented and agreed with God about my situation. The next day God spoke to me to give $400 to a man when I only had $800 in my checking account. At the time, payroll was due and was about $5,000. Even though it seemed very foolish, I wrote the check and God performed a miracle.

When I gave the man the money, he started weeping. He explained, "Just this morning I asked God for $400." Whether payroll would have been paid or not, I sensed that I had heard the voice of God, which was worth the $400 to me.

To me and those around me, my actions appeared *foolish*. From God's perspective, they were *obedient*, I made payroll that month, and within a year and a half, my business was completely out of debt. Also most of my employees came to the Lord after I repented of debt and invited Christ's kingdom into my business.

Communist country opens to God's kingdom

On the trip to Mongolia I mentioned earlier, God prompted my friend and me to anoint with oil the corners of the government square in the capitol city. Our guide (more like a guard) was wondering what we were doing with the oil.

We went to a platform at the center of the square and declared, "One day we will preach the gospel from this spot." Within six months God called us to return and we preached the gospel in that square. At the time I did not realize this was a prophetic act.

Our weakness shows God's strength

Prophetic acts are hearing the voice of God and acting on what He tells us to do. Prophetic acts usually look weak and foolish in the natural. However, the Bible says God has chosen the foolish things of the world to shame the wise and the weak things of the world to shame the strong (1 Corinthians 1:27). Hearing God's voice and acting, even though it may feel weak or foolish, is powerful in God's sight.

You don't have to be a super hero

When you hear the voice of the Lord and move in faith to do what He says, you will see God move. I'm not that talented, but when I hear from God, I can do anything.

I've given a few examples from the Bible and you can find more prophetic acts throughout the Scriptures. God speaks to someone, he or she obeys, and God shows up. You can follow this example also.

If you want to see the supernatural come into the marketplace, all you have to do is act on what God is telling you to do. At the time it might seem very peculiar, weak, and foolish. Hearing and obeying can seem hit or miss. But God has faithfully come on the scene many, many times as I've acted upon what I believe He has said to me. When God's super shows up, our natural quickly has to take a back seat.

God's super will come to our natural

We bring the super to the natural by listening to the voice of the Lord and following obediently. Every time He tells me to do something I think is foolish, I know His power is right around the corner. When God speaks to you about praying for people or blessing them, you'll never see miracles or signs and wonders unless you obey what the Spirit of the Lord is telling you to do.

If you think you can do it in the natural, you'll only get a natural result. However, if you obey when you hear the voice of the Lord, you'll get a spiritual, supernatural result.

Fear warns us that the enemy is on the scene

Hearing God's voice and stepping out in faith can be scary. Just know that when you fear, the devil is near. The devil uses fear to stop God's work through you.

The God factor conquers the fear factor

Our God is a God of faith, not fear. The Bible says it's impossible to please God without faith (Hebrews 11:6). Faith comes by hearing the word of God, or may I say the *voice* of God (Romans 10:17). So when we know that we have heard God's voice, we have faith to act upon His word.

Don't fear when you hear

The Bible says only those who do the will of the Father will enter the kingdom of heaven. Jesus said many will stand before Him at the end of time and say, "Lord, we did many wonderful things in Your name." Jesus' reply will be, "I never knew you." Who is Jesus talking about when He says this? He's talking about those who did their own thing thinking their good deeds gained them favor with God. God only wants us to humble ourselves, trust Him, listen to His voice, and obey (Proverbs 3:5-6; Isaiah 66:2).

The only thing we need to fear is not hearing God. Jesus said, "My sheep hear My voice, and I know them, and they follow Me" (John 10:27). If you have a relationship with Jesus Christ, you do hear His voice.

Step out in faith to see God's super in your natural

The Lord once asked me to pray for a great big guy. I walked up to him and said. "The Lord told me to pray for you." He looked down at me and said, "What about?" I looked at him and said sheepishly, "I don't know." He looked back at me and said, "I know what you're supposed to pray for me about." He told me that his wife had just left him that morning. So I prayed that the Lord would help him.

I had no idea what was going on in this guy's life, but I knew the Lord wanted me to pray for him. I did and he was blessed.

God's kingdom advances when we hear and obey

The true test of hearing the voice of God is if the kingdom of God is moved forward. Whatever we do, wherever we go, whomever we talk to, God wants us to bring His kingdom in that place, to those people. Every time I look at the result of my actions, if I didn't release the kingdom of

God in some way (like praying, blessing, or encouraging with God's word), I didn't do the job.

Our main objective should be to bring God's kingdom. You may not understand what He's asking you to do. That's OK. You don't need to understand. You just need to do it. If you will, one day you will hear, "Well done, good and faithful servant." When you hear God's voice and obey, there will be much joy in your life here on earth and for eternity.

Don't tell me you don't hear God. You're hearing Him right now. What's He saying to you? What has He told you to do that you haven't done? What is He telling you to do that you need to do right now?

Right now God's telling me to pray for you

In the name of Jesus Christ, I pray that you would know you can hear God's voice. I pray that you would listen to what God says through the Bible, in your spirit, through other trusted followers of Christ, in dreams or visions, or whatever way God chooses to speak to you. I ask that God will give you courage to obey immediately and wisdom to know how to carry out what He's told you to do. I ask that you will be filled with much joy about what God does and that you give Him the credit for His work through you. Amen.

There's work to do

Matthew 9:37 says, "The harvest is plentiful, but the workers are few." It was only a few who were accused of turning the world upside down in the early church (see Acts

17:6). The Lord recently woke me out of my sleep and said, "Stop believing that the workers are few. That was two thousand years ago. Today I have millions of people going to work every day in the harvest fields. The problem is that they don't know why they are there."

God's will for your life is to advance the kingdom of God wherever you go. The Great Commission says, "Go!" Go to school, go to work, go to the city, go to the nations. God is transforming the marketplace today as more Christians understand that their workplace is God's harvest field, not just the place to make a living. Read on to understand more clearly what your role in the kingdom of God looks like and how to join with others to turn your world upside down.

Take Action

- Advance God's kingdom by developing a history of listening to what He says and responding in obedience. (See 2 Corinthians 10:3-7.)

- Don't fear when you hear. When God speaks, it is an invitation into a relationship and an adventure with Him. (See 2 Timothy 1:7-10.)

- When the Lord asks you to do something, look at what He can do, not at your shortcomings. With God, all things are possible. (See Matthew 19:26; Philippians 4:12-13.)

Five Yards and a Cloud of Dust

*Advancing God's kingdom is a full-contact sport. When two
kingdoms collide, there will be a clash and a whole lot of dust.*

I grew up in southern Minnesota in a small farm town.
Football was my game and I was the running back on my
high school's varsity team. When the team was in a difficult
situation for their next down, the coach would say, "Hochreiter, we need five yards and a cloud of dust." It was always
a struggle to make that five yards, but very satisfying when I
did, especially when I saw the smile on the coach's face.

I played football because I liked the toughness of the game and the satisfaction of winning. As I grew older, whether in the Marines, working for another employer, or running my own business, my desire to win remained strong.

We learn how to win from others

I used to play racquetball with a guy who would contest every point I scored. I asked him one day, "Why do you antagonize me with complaints when you know the point was good? He said, "That's how I win games. I wear down my opponents mentally and physically." This was his practice because that's the way he was taught to win.

My first real job coming out of the Marine Corps was with a fabric company. My employer trained me to run the business shrewdly. The textile industry standard was that you could deduct a percentage for flaws in the fabric. We tried to deduct as much as we could get away with, even if there wasn't a good reason. A discount on the bill added to our bottom line.

When we got the fabric back to our factory to cut into pieces and sell, we would run the machines at a fast rate. This process would stretch the fabric some so we would get a little more out of it. Only someone clever would notice they weren't getting as much out of the fabric.

I learned to take advantage of people because that's what it took to win. At the time, it seemed like the right thing to do so we could make money. I watched my boss take the company from unprofitable to profitable using these business practices.

Winning at all costs isn't God's way

After eight years of working for this company, I started my own business. I had come to Christ years earlier, but when I started my own company, my relationship with the Lord was deepening.

I had learned to tell customers that I could deliver an order in two weeks when I knew it would take four. I would tell them whatever I needed to get the business. As the conviction of the Holy Spirit came into my company, I saw that this wasn't God's way for business. I wanted to run my company in a godly way.

Change takes a cloud of dust

When I started to change the way I did business, I could no longer rely on the business practices I had learned. I almost went broke because I was being honest. I would tell a customer, "I can't get that order out in two weeks," and I would lose their business. I remember one of the buyers saying to me, "Why don't you just lie to me so I can give you the business." It's amazing how acceptable it was in the market to lie, but I would respond, "I can't do that."

Even though the transition was difficult, I decided it was better to do what was right than to succeed in an ungodly way. This was my entry point into leading my company in God's ways. Once God was honored in my business by running it according to His purposes, we did become successful. More importantly, we advanced the kingdom of God in the marketplace.

Jesus wants you to do what He did

Have you ever seen someone wearing a wristband that has "WWJD" on it? Maybe you wear one so you can remind yourself "What Would Jesus Do?" when you face difficult situations in life. To be Christ-like is supposed to be the goal of every Christian.

Being Christ-like is more than being a moral person who tries hard to demonstrate the fruit of the Spirit (Galatians 5:22-23). God's plan is that we walk in both the fullness of Christ's character and in His power. Being Christ-like also means that we go and cast out demons, heal the sick, fast and pray, weep over the condition of cities, tell a storm to be quiet, feed a bunch of hungry people with just a little bit of food, raise the dead, and advance the kingdom in the marketplace just like Jesus did.

When the kingdom comes, all hell breaks loose

When things got tough in my business, it was the start of something good. When all hell breaks loose in your life, it isn't necessarily a bad thing. In God's hands, a clash of kingdoms (our way of doing things vs. God's way) will bring good results: wrong thinking is challenged and corrected; demonic strongholds are broken; bad habits are replaced with new, healthier, more godly ways of living.

Advancing the kingdom is a full-contact sport and significant progress doesn't happen without a cloud of dust. In the life of Jesus and His early followers there was conflict and persecution when the kingdom of God clashed with the kingdom of darkness. You can expect the same (Matthew 24:4-13).

If you have been born again into the kingdom of God, you've been born into a battle. We cannot let the price tag of victory intimidate us into backing down or giving up before we see a breakthrough. Jesus Christ won the ultimate victory to return authority to those who follow Him. It's up to us to enforce Christ's work and bring His kingdom wherever we go until He returns. Jesus said, "In this world you will have trouble. But take heart! I have overcome the world" (John 16:33).

Jesus has a reward for those who overcome

There are many blessings when we follow King Jesus and advance His kingdom's business. Some bonuses we receive on earth. Other rewards we will receive in heaven. Our job is to overcome and advance the kingdom, help others to do the same, and send any glory that comes our way to God (Matthew 5:3-12; James 1:12).

Next let's see what it looks like to live the kingdom way—how Jesus and His followers advanced the kingdom of God and taught others to do the same.

Take Action

- Get out of the locker room and onto the playing field to win the game. God doesn't just want you to go to church; He wants you to *be* the Church.

- Expect a cloud of dust to make progress in the kingdom of God. Jesus warned us that in this world we would experience trouble. But He said, "Take heart! I have overcome the world." If you're facing trouble, take some time to consider God's grace to overcome your present situation. (See John 16:33; Hebrews 12:4; Revelation 3:7-13.)

Living the Kingdom Way

—————

Jesus changed the lives of those He encountered. Living the kingdom
way always leaves your world different than you found it.

If you had to summarize the ministry of Jesus, Matthew 9:35-36 would be a good place to go. It says Jesus went through all the cities and villages, taught in synagogues, proclaimed the good news of the kingdom, and healed every disease and sickness. When He saw people, He felt compassion for them and reached out to help them. This is what advancing the kingdom looked like for Jesus.

The apostle John wrote, "The reason the Son of God appeared was to destroy the devil's work" (1 John 3:8). As Jesus advanced His kingdom, He was destroying the works of the enemy.

Jesus sent His disciples out to do the same thing. Matthew 10 records that Jesus called His twelve disciples to Him and gave them authority to drive out evil spirits and heal every disease and sickness. He then sent them out and said, "As you go, preach this message: 'The kingdom of heaven is near.' Heal the sick, raise the dead, cleanse those who have leprosy, drive out demons. Freely you have received, freely give."

Jesus went on to warn them that they would be arrested, flogged by the religious institutions, and brought before governors and kings to be witnesses. Because of Jesus, they would be betrayed, be put to death by loved ones, and be hated by all men. Jesus concluded, "Those who stand firm to the end, will be saved" (Matthew 10:17-22). Advancing the kingdom according to Jesus takes courage and brings persecution.

An example in the life of Jesus

Luke 8:26-39 shows us an example of advancing the kingdom Jesus' way.

Jesus was in the marketplace and ran across a man full of demons and controlled by the kingdom of darkness. These demons gave him supernatural strength so that no one could subdue him. He had often been bound but he tore the chains apart and broke the irons off his feet. When Jesus showed up, the demons reacted to the Son of God and begged Him not to torture them or kick them out of the region but send them into nearby pigs. The pigs lost and Jesus set the man free.

When the people from the town heard what happened, they didn't rush out to say, "Hey thanks, that guy was a real mess and we're glad because now he can be a good citizen." Instead they told Jesus to get out of town. When Jesus started to leave, the man begged to go with Jesus. Jesus said, "Go home to your family and tell them how much the Lord has done for you, and how he has had mercy on you." The man went away and in many cities told how much Jesus had done for him.

An example from the life of the apostle Paul

Acts 16:16-40 shows how the apostle Paul and his companion, Silas, stirred up their share of dust moving the kingdom of God forward when they were in the city of Philippi.

While in the marketplace, Paul and Silas ran into a slave girl who had a spirit that enabled her to foretell the future. After a few days of getting harassed by this spirit, Paul turned to the girl and said, "In the name of Jesus Christ I command you to come out of her!"

When the girl's owners realized they had lost their source of income, they dragged Paul and Silas to face the authorities. Paul and Silas were accused of throwing the city into an uproar. The judges had them stripped, severely beaten, and thrown in prison.

While Paul and Silas were singing praises to God that night, there was suddenly a major earthquake. The Bible says the foundations of the prison were shaken, all the doors were opened, and everyone's chains came loose. This was great news for the prisoners, but bad news for the guy guarding them. The jailer drew his sword and was about to kill himself.

At that moment Paul shouted, "Do not harm yourself, for we are all here!" The Bible says that "the jailer rushed in and fell trembling before Paul and Silas." He asked, "What must I do to be saved?" They replied, "Believe in the Lord Jesus, and you will be saved – you and your household."

Through this story we can see that:

- Paul and Silas brought the kingdom of God into the marketplace in Philippi.
- A clash occurred and a girl was set free from an evil spirit.
- Paul and Silas got beaten up badly and were thrown in prison, but they brought the kingdom there too.
- Another clash occurred as they sang, but this time the outcome was salvation not just for a suicidal jailer, but also for his entire family.
- It is likely that this family became a part of the early Church and helped others to come into God's kingdom just like they did.

God wants to show you a better way

Not everyone likes the freedom God can bring. The townspeople couldn't handle the demonic encounter, but the man freed from the demons was so thrilled he told everyone around what Jesus did for him. The owners of the slave girl didn't like losing out on big profits. However, the jailer eagerly welcomed the better way of life that Paul and Silas offered him.

If you are in a difficult situation right now, God wants to show you a better way. Just know that His way through Jesus Christ will bring a shaking. This is so hell can break loose, the doors fly open, and your chains fall off. Paul and Silas began to sing in their prison cell. Do the same in the midst of your trial and watch the kingdom of God advance against the gates of hell in your life and bust them wide open. Consider it pure joy because the devil hates it when we praise God.

Examples today

The New Testament is filled with examples of Jesus and His followers pressing through serious opposition to advance the kingdom of God and then teaching others to do the same. Sometimes it's easy to look at the Bible and say, "Well, that was for them. But things are different now."

So I'd like to share with you a few stories that show how followers of Jesus are advancing the kingdom of God today.

Bob's story: Becoming a marketplace Padre

Bob was born again into the kingdom of God in 1997 at the age of 55. At the time he was the sales/service manager for a textile services company. He supervised 17 truck drivers and two salesmen.

In Bob's words,

I was the ringleader of a very rowdy crew. I was the chief sinner and proud of it! As the boss, I was a tough disciplinarian, but at the same time, fair. My guys responded to my leadership. They were commissioned drivers and I helped them make a lot of money. This led to team harmony.

On the day I got saved, I knew my sinful behavior had to stop. I repented and begged God's Holy Spirit to truly change me. With God's help, I threw away the ashtrays in the office, poured out the bottle of hard liquor in my desk, and cleaned up my filthy mouth. Pornographic magazines were replaced with Bibles. I was serious about following Jesus and was not ashamed of the gospel. Instead of cursing and judging, I prayed and blessed. My coworkers thought I had lost it and were understandably upset. They liked the old Bob.

Within a few weeks, God started working in the hearts of some of my fellow workers. When they saw that my heart change was real, they began to relax around me and ask questions about Jesus. I worked there another 2 ½ years, and through the wisdom and power of the Holy Spirit, many workers accepted the Lord and God's kingdom was advanced in my company.

My general manager did not like the changes he saw in me. I had been his right-hand man until Christ began to change my life. My business tactics changed and I wouldn't do anything unless I knew God would approve. Things got very uncomfortable. He tried to fire me, but the company wouldn't let him.

I had a burning desire to minister in the marketplace, but I had gone as far as I could go at this company. So after twenty years, I left a healthy 401(k), and all the perks and security I had enjoyed for so long. I knew the Lord would provide."

So in August of 2000, Bob was hired as a salesman for a linen company that specializes in providing linen for hospitals and related healthcare facilities. It was the lowest sales job in the company. But Bob started praying and blessing. Bob continues his story.

I made it totally clear to my general manager, his office staff, and his plant managers and workers that God was my boss and my main goal was to further the kingdom of God in that plant. The sales part of my new job went extremely well. God's hand was in every business contact I made. In my first five months, I exceeded my quota by 500 percent. I ended the year 2000 as the number one sales person in the company and continued near the top of the list all four years I was employed there.

In the California linen plant, 99 percent of the workers were born in Mexico. They were extremely hard working and family oriented. My first feeble attempts at sharing Christ with them seemed futile. I tried to speak to them in English or with my limited Spanish. Neither worked and I was disappointed. But I never gave up. God sent me there to further His kingdom and that was going to happen! I continued to seek God's wisdom.

I began to pray with other prayer warrior buddies early in the morning on a daily basis. To no one's surprise, God started moving in that linen plant. He revealed to me that I needed to recruit Spanish-speaking interpreters, and so I did. I found them among the first people who came to know Christ.

The Holy Spirit led me to eat with the workers, spend break time with them, pray, laugh, and cry with them. I was "Roberto" and I was one of them. They knew I really cared for them. I started by praying with one lady in the garment department on my first day. This grew to praying with over 200 people weekly.

I was never once warned or told to lighten up. The general manager always encouraged me to continue. In fact, he made many opportunities available to minister to his employees. He loved the favor God was giving to his plant.

As time passed, the workers started to call me "Papa," "Padre," or "Don Roberto." When it came time for me to retire in 2004, I was officially named 'Chaplain.' I continue to pray with the workers, management staff, plus two corporate vice presidents who visit regularly. I also visit injured workers in the hospital and at home. Many times there are 20 to 30 prayer requests waiting for me. I have five to ten interpreters available on any given day to help.

Every desk in the plant has a Bible on it. God's Word is readily available; it gets read and discussed daily. Thousands of people have received prayer and over one hundred have come to know the Lord and are now regularly attending local congregations. The first woman who was given a Bible is on her third consecutive year of reading it from cover to cover. I am welcomed with open arms not only in this company, but also in other companies where I am allowed to minister and make kingdom disciples.

Through Bob's story we can see that:

- Bob had the mindset to minister in the marketplace immediately after his conversion.

- Bob experienced opposition and struggled as the kingdom of God clashed with the kingdom of darkness.

- As he prayed, he saw God's power and blessing come to employees and entire companies.

- Because of Bob's life, others are learning to walk with Jesus.

- Bob's disciples are in turn praying and blessing others and are making their own kingdom disciples.

My story

I shared earlier how I began to disciple my company to be a godly company that would bring honor to the Lord. At the time we were having every kind of problem. We had borrowed heavily to try to capture the bicycle clothing market. We succeeded in capturing much of the market share, but the market shifted overnight, sales stopped, and we were left with a ton of inventory that wasn't worth much. I went to every supplier and asked for mercy while we straightened things out.

Earlier in this book I shared how God spoke to me and told me to repent of debt. God also led me to give $400 to a guy when I did not have enough money to make payroll. I remember sitting my employees down to tell them I was turning the company over to God. I asked them to forgive me for running the company into the ground. They thought I had lost it.

I didn't have a clue about what was going to happen. We were hundreds of thousands of dollars in debt and had no way to dig ourselves out. I prayed, "Lord, you have to show me what to do and I'll do whatever it takes."

I told the Lord, "I'll file bankruptcy." He responded, "I haven't told you to file, I've told you to stand and I'll be with you." Two verses in the Bible that became very meaningful to me during this time were Matthew 6:33 and Romans 8:28:

> But seek first his kingdom and his righteousness, and all these things will be given to you as well.

> And we know that in all things God works for the good of those who love him, who have been called according to his purpose.

These verses encouraged me because I knew that even if I really messed up, God could work things out because I loved Him and was seeking His purposes.

I talked to the suppliers and leveled with those around me, "We're out of money and we're going to trust God." I prayed with my employees and asked God to lead the company.

My inventory included a bunch of fabric with bad color worth thousands of dollars. No one wanted it. I prayed and asked God what to do with it. Within a short time, a guy showed up and wanted that specific color. All the employees saw this happen. Machinery would break down and I couldn't afford a mechanic. My employees knew the machine was broken, they would see me pray, and the next minute the machine was running. Everyone knew I didn't know how to fix it.

In the morning my lead manager, Sharon, a few of my lead workers and I would pray together. Employees saw God begin to move in the company and wanted to know Him. It wasn't through my preaching; they saw us praying and asked God for guidance.

The company began to succeed as I put things in order. People who wouldn't pay their bills started to pay. When my vendors saw me begin to pay my bills and knew I would be honest with them, they started to work with me. I would also get to pray for them and encourage them.

We built relationships with them and they started to believe in us. They knew I had integrity and that we weren't going to take them. I told them, "God is helping us," and they would say, "We need help too." Then they would see stuff happen in their companies. I learned that the kingdom of God is advanced through relationships, and discipling my company simply meant I did what was right before the Lord and others (Matthew 22:34-40).

During this time the Lord told me to give the motorcycle division of the company to one of our distributors. It was the only part of our company that was making money. This guy was a "paint peeler," which means that John could speak to the wall, and because his language was so foul, the paint would fall off. We had put hundreds of thousands of dollars into marketing our name and had some recognition in the market. But I could see that the manufacturing part of our industry was going to go overseas in the near future.

I called John up and told him what God had said to me. He replied, "God really told you that?!?" I said, "If you buy the inventory at cost, I'll give you the name, the patterns, and all you need to manufacture." This had no benefit to me other than the Lord told me to do it. He thought it was a trick.

It took a number of months to make the transition. Soon after that John called from Las Vegas at 3:00 a.m. and told me, "You're not going to believe what happened. I gave my life to Jesus." Even though John came out from under the curse, he had a rough time. He also owed me a lot of money because of the inventory he bought. I told him I would take $100 off his debt for every hour he would read the Bible.

(John persevered through some really tough times and went on to become very successful and influential in the United States motorcycle industry. He has brought God's kingdom into this market like no one else. He's an announcer and goes to all the national races. Many of the people he encourages, including the racers, have come to know and follow Christ.)

When I gave this part of the company away, I had no clue what I was going to do in the future. I ended up having to lay off a guy I led to the Lord. He got a job at a sunglasses company that was small at the time. One day he called me and said, "If you can find this specialized lens-cleaning fabric, you can get a big order from us." Having many contacts in the fabric industry I thought, "I can find this fabric." I looked for about six months and couldn't find it.

I had given a good portion of the business away to John and was finishing up what business we had. We were very close to being out of debt, but it looked like I might have to close the company. The few people who were still working for me were praying daily for God to help us to find this fabric.

One day a guy from Las Vegas called me on the phone: "There's a ski show in town and I think you need to come." Rick, one of my employees who was very committed to the Lord, encouraged me to go. So we went to Las Vegas. On the way I prayed, "Lord, if you want me to be a janitor somewhere, that's OK. I just want to serve you. If this is the end of the company, so be it."

The convention center was full of vendors. I said to Rick, "I don't know where we should even start to look for this stuff." So we sat at a table and prayed. When we got done a lady who had been observing us asked, "Were you doing what I thought you were doing?" I said, "Well, if you thought we were praying, we were." She continued, "What were you praying for?" We told her about the fabric and she pointed us to the right section of the convention center.

We spent a good part of the day in that section of the convention center talking to vendors and trying to find this fabric. We eventually got discouraged. It was getting late and we needed to go. Apparently God was seeing if we would be obedient. As we walked toward the door to leave, Rick saw a company from Japan and said, "I think we need to go talk to them." We walked in and handed the fabric sample to a guy in a suit. He gave the fabric to a sales guy who said, "We don't have this fabric." The guy in the suit handed the fabric back to me with his business card and said, "I know where to get this fabric."

This guy happened to be the only person in the United States who represented this special fabric. He was flying from New York to Los Angeles and had briefly stopped in Las Vegas to see a friend. It was a divine appointment. The rest of this story is told in Thank God It's Monday by Rick Heeren.[1] The bottom line is that we ended up getting $10 million in business from the sunglasses company.

Shortly after we got this deal, the Lord started speaking to me about taking the kingdom of God to nations that hadn't been reached with the gospel of Christ. We began to pray for unreached people groups and for opportunities. We didn't know what that would look like. God's desire was that I would use the money he was giving me to take Christ into hard-to-reach nations. One of those countries was Mongolia.

Mongolia

I learned there were only a few people in Mongolia who knew God at that time. So my company began to invest in that country. On one of our trips I remember crying out to God, "Why don't these people get saved?" We had been preaching for five days in a college class about how Jesus had come to earth so we could know God and be reconciled to Him. They said, "That's a great story but we're Buddhist."

We went back to the hotel and asked the Lord, "What is the problem?" The Lord showed us we needed to pray for the sick and demonstrate that God is not just a God of words but also a God of power (1 Corinthians 2:4-5).

The next day we went back to pray for the sick. We shared the gospel message and asked if anyone was sick. One girl had come with a severe flu because she was not allowed to miss one class. Everyone knew she was sick and pointed at her. Reluctantly she came to the front for prayer. After we prayed for her she started to scream, "I'm hot! I'm hot!" The Lord had healed her. Others in the classroom immediately streamed up front for prayer. At the end of the week, we baptized 36 people who became the first believers in the history of the country.

We talked until we were blue in the face with no fruit. But when we prayed for them, God's kingdom was established and advanced.

Back in California

When I tell my story, it can sound like, "We were in tough times, we turned things over to God, things got better, and now everything is great." The truth is that we went through many hard times. I had many sleepless nights. It took everything I had to do what needed to be done. Others in my company had to persevere in their own way too.

Sharon, my lead manager, was the first one to get saved in my company. All hell immediately broke loose in her life. Her husband told her he wanted a divorce. He had a girlfriend and he was leaving. She was devastated.

Before she received Christ she was really mean. But as her husband was leaving, she told him that she really loved him. He gave her the divorce papers anyway and got married to his girlfriend.

Sharon told us, "I still love my husband and I'm praying for him." She didn't pray that they would break up but that they would be happy and come to know the Lord. She would tell me, "Someday I believe we'll be married again." Sharon never gave up on him. She believed for the best.

He and his new wife couldn't get along and did break up. Through the trouble he came to know the Lord and remarried Sharon. Sharon became a huge part of what God did in the company and in my life.

None of the wins were easy, but God was always with us. He trained us to disciple the company to do what was right even when it hurt. We were willing to do that. We had to kick the hell out of our company – all the demonic forces that were keeping us from advancing the kingdom in the United States' marketplace and then around the world. As we started to believe God, a trail of signs and wonders followed us. Major impact in the nations of the world today can be traced to our humble efforts to hear and obey God.

In my story you can see how:

- God gave grace to a broken company and used us as we pushed through the cloud of dust to win the marketplace for the kingdom of God.
- God blesses us as we began to honor Him in simple, tangible ways.
- We listened to what God was saying and obeyed, even when it was really hard.
- Our scope of discipleship went from individuals, to companies, to industries, to nations of the world.

What is your role?

The last verse of the book of Acts describes what the apostle Paul was doing late in his life. Here's a guy whose life and writing shaped the early Church and are still influencing our world today. Of all the things he could have been doing, he chose to preach the kingdom of God and point people to King Jesus (Acts 28:31). I believe that this is what God wants from us as well.

Now let's look at what your role looks like as a kingdom disciple in the kingdom of God.

Take Action

- Take a look once again at the main points that are taken from the stories in this chapter. Which can you relate to and why?

- What kind of results do you want to see in your own life?
- Ask God to show you what fully "living the kingdom way" can look like for you. What is He showing you?

Your Role in God's Kingdom

Jesus came to destroy the works of the enemy.
Since God made you to be Christ-like, He expects you
to do the same as you walk in His character and power.

It's easy to confuse what it means to be a Christian. The term "Christian" was first used in Antioch, Syria, to describe those who followed Jesus and advanced His kingdom (Acts 11:26). If we take on the name "Christian," we need to take on the behavior of those who were first called Christians. Unfortunately we've strayed away from that original definition. Because of this, I prefer to use the term "kingdom disciple" to refer to someone who follows Christ.

Your role in the kingdom of God is to be a disciple of the King. A kingdom disciple is a person who wants to think and act like King Jesus and is willing to lay down his or her life for the kingdom. Being Christ-like is not isolating certain *characteristics* of Jesus and trying to be a good person. It means knowing the *character*—the person—of Jesus and embracing all of Him completely.

Kingdom disciples actively follow King Jesus

When I started out in business, I was "discipled," or trained, to do business a certain way. My boss was the king and trained me to advance his kingdom his way. He then expected me to teach others how to do the same.

Kingdom disciples are those who have been trained to advance God's kingdom wherever they go and teach others to do the same. Kingdom disciples:

- Know how Jesus and the early apostles lived and seek to live in the same way.
- Measure the impact of their Christian activities in "kingdom" terms and pioneer beyond the boundaries or walls of a religious institution.
- Compete against the devil, not against other Christians.
- See a bigger picture—entire companies, industries, cities, and nations being reached for Christ.

- Seek and build God's kingdom, not their own.

- Know that the role of church ministers is to equip them for the work of the ministry in the marketplace and the world.

- Listen to what the Lord is saying and obey.

- Bring the kingdom wherever they go because they know that if they are full-time Christians, they are in full-time ministry.

- Operate in the mindset that "these signs shall follow those who believe" (Mark 16:17).

- Go after both sides of the coin: fullness of the character of Christ and fullness of the power of the Spirit.

How to be a Kingdom disciple

There are four parts to what it means to be a kingdom disciple.

1. Enter the kingdom of God personally.

The first step toward being a kingdom disciple is to be born into the kingdom of God. You do that by repenting. The first sermon Jesus preached was, "Repent, for the kingdom of heaven is near" (Matthew 4:17). Repent means to *stop* going your own way, *turn* 180 degrees, and *begin to follow* King Jesus. Entering the kingdom of God is entering into all of who King Jesus is—His *character* and His *power*.

In the chapter "God's 30-Day Curse-back Guarantee," I talk about how to come out from under the curse of sin and death through faith in Jesus Christ. Jesus said, "No one can see the kingdom of God unless he is born again" (John 3:3). If you have not been born again, you are in a different kingdom and under the curse.

Pray with me: *Father God, forgive me for ruling my own kingdom and rejecting you as the true and only King. I give you the throne of my life and turn away from doing my own thing. Come and rule over me, over all that I am and all that I have, and lead me in your paths. Fill me with your Holy Spirit and come upon me with your power to be a witness for you kingdom's sake. Amen.*

2. Seek first the kingdom of God.

How do you measure your walk with the Lord? A number of years ago a friend of mine spent a year in Moscow, Russia, as an exchange English teacher in a public school. The principal told David, "We know when you are in the building. We can feel the difference." In her own way she was saying that the Holy Spirit's presence was tangible as David brought the kingdom of God with him to school each day.

As he was heading back to the United States, he ran into a church group that had just finished a two-week outreach in northern Russia. When they found out that David had just spent a year in Moscow, they asked him, "How many people did you see get saved?" David hadn't "prayed the prayer" with anyone. It was a few months before he could see that his time in Moscow had any positive effect whatsoever.

Kingdom success is not about how many people you "get saved." God is the one who draws people to repentance

(John 6:44; Romans 2:4). Our fruitfulness is determined by our love for God and how faithful we are to do what the Holy Spirit asks us to do each day (John 14-15:17).

The kingdom of God is also not about trying harder to be a good person. God simply asks us to seek Him and do what He says. God's kingdom gets advanced when we see what God is already doing around us and cooperate with Him (John 5:19; 8:28). This is what Jesus did and He was fruitful. You can do this and be just as fruitful (John 14:10-14).

The Bible says that God determined where and when you would live. "God did this so that [you] would seek him" (Acts 17:24-27). Seeking God means cultivating a relationship with Him, just like you would another person. Jesus said our love for Him will motivate us to obey His word. The result is that God makes His home within us so we can abide with Him in the most intimate places of our lives (John 14:15-21).

Seeking His kingdom also means that our priorities are focused on the right things. As we seek first God and His kingdom, then all the other things are added (Matthew 6:33). When we are seeking God, we hear his voice. When we hear God's voice and do what He says, God's super comes into our natural, like we talked about earlier in this book. We can be fruitful every day of our lives if we'll seek God first, listen to the Holy Spirit's leading, and then bring the kingdom of God wherever we go.

Pray with me: *Father God, I want my life to count and I know that true success starts by seeking you first. Reveal yourself*

to me in the everyday circumstances of life, my job, and family.
Help me to get my priorities in the right order. I want you to be
first place. Make your home within me and help me to hear you
clearly and respond to what you say. Amen.

3. Have courage to face the clash.

Advancing God's kingdom is a full-contact sport. When two kingdoms collide, there will be a clash and a whole lot of dust.

Besides Jesus, Paul was probably the most beat-up guy in the Bible (2 Corinthians 11:25-28). One time, a crowd stoned Paul and dragged him outside the city thinking he was dead. So what did Paul do? He got up and headed back into the city. The next day he headed to another city to strengthen the disciples and encourage them to remain true to the faith. He told other Christians, "We must go through many hardships to enter the kingdom of God" (Acts 14:19-22).

Other disciples responded to hardship in the same way. After Peter and John were threatened not to talk about Jesus, they prayed, "Now Lord, consider their threats and enable your servants to speak your word with great boldness. Stretch out your hand to heal and perform miraculous signs and wonders through the name of your holy servant Jesus." After they prayed, the place where they were meeting was shaken. They were all filled with the Holy Spirit and spoke the word of God boldly (Acts 4:1-31). The clash did not cause them to back down. It caused them to cry out to the Lord for courage.

A clash of kingdoms is inevitable. Jesus said that you will have trouble and you will be hated (John 16:33; Matthew 10:22). Be ready for it. When it happens, pray, "Lord, grant me boldness." Just like the apostle Paul, get up, dust yourself off, and head back into the marketplace.

Jesus said you could tell that the kingdom of God has come upon you when you see demons being driven out by the Spirit of God (Matthew 12:25-28). These evil spirits compete for our attention and want to fill our minds with evil things. We need to kick them out and replace them with God's thoughts (Philippians 4:6-8).

Advancing the kingdom is driving out the darkness and releasing God's character and power wherever we go. This is Christianity at its fullest. Most of the early disciples were martyred for living in this way. They knew their mission, tenaciously pursued it, and saw their future reward.

If you need an incentive to persevere through the clash, remember your reward. Jesus said, "Blessed are you when men hate you, when they exclude you and insult you and reject your name as evil, because of the Son of Man (Jesus). Rejoice in that day and leap for joy, because great is your reward in heaven" (Luke 6:22-23). If you have five minutes right now, read the second and third chapters of Revelation in the Bible. These chapters record the words that Jesus spoke to John to pass along to the churches. At the end of each of the letters you will see what Jesus says He will do for those who overcome (2:7, 11, 17, 25-29; 3-5, 11-12, 21). God's blessings are for us right now on earth, and eternal rewards await those who overcome knowing that "with God we will gain the victory" (Psalm 60:12; 108:13).

Pray with me: *Jesus, thank you that you won a decisive victory over Satan through your life, death, and resurrection. Grant me the courage I need to experience your victory each day as I advance your kingdom wherever I go. Give me your strength to get up when I'm knocked down, and your rest when I'm tired. Through you I can live valiantly. Through it all, help me to keep my eyes on you – my reward. Amen.*

4. Give away what you have received.

When Jesus sent out his disciples to preach "the kingdom of heaven is near," He told them to "heal the sick, raise the dead, cleanse those who have leprosy, drive out demons." Then He added, "Freely you have received, freely give" (Matthew 10:7-8). The last part of what it means to be a kingdom disciple is to give away what you have freely received.

Next let's talk about how to give away what God has given to us, win the marketplace for King Jesus, and train others to do the same.

Take Action

- Look back at the four parts of what it means to be a kingdom disciple. How you are actively following King Jesus?
- What area would you like to grow in? Why?
- What are a few things you want to do this week to start growing in this area?

7

How to Win
the Marketplace
for King Jesus

Jesus won an eternal victory alone, but He doesn't expect us to win the
marketplace all by ourselves. Christ is the Head, and those who follow
Him are to work in harmony as His body to get the job done.

Kingdom discipleship deliberately points each disciple's love, attention, and service back to the King Himself to foster a living relationship with Him. As the disciple abides in Christ and responds to Him (because they are taught to seek Him first), Christ in return pours His life into them creating a very life-giving cycle. Because of this, kingdom disciples reproduce in the likeness of the King and His kingdom.

So if you're a kingdom disciple, how can you proactively disciple others to become kingdom disciples too? By pointing to the King and His kingdom every chance you get.

Let's look at four things you can do to help others come into the kingdom of God and walk in the ways of King Jesus. I will also include a few practical steps you can take to walk out each of these areas.

1. Position yourself in the model of Luke 10

Luke 10 tells the story of Jesus sending out seventy of His followers into every place He was about to go. Jesus wants to send you where He wants His kingdom to be established. Jesus said the harvest is plentiful, but the workers are few. The only reason the workers are few today is because many are inside the locker room (the church building) thinking it's the playing field.

"Position yourself in the model of Luke 10" means you're in the game listening to the Coach ready to be a part of the next play. You see that the harvest is plentiful where you live and work and that God is sending you into the fields where He wants His kingdom to be advanced. Wherever you are, Jesus wants you to:

1. Speak peace and bless.
2. Build caring relationships with others.

3. Pray for felt needs.

4. Show how the kingdom of God has come near.[2]

Let's look at each in a little more detail.

Speak peace and bless, don't curse (Luke 10:5)

When Jesus sent His followers out, He warned them that there would be wolves out there (Luke 10:3). A great reason to position yourself as a peacemaker and as one who blesses.

Earlier we talked about "blessing busters." One blessing buster is the belief that God only wants to bless some people, not everyone. Jesus came that all would have the opportunity to be blessed. God wants us to demonstrate His heart and be a blessing to those around us, even to those who curse us (Luke 6:27-28).

Build relationships, don't avoid them (Luke 10:7-8)

Jesus told His followers not to move around from house to house but to stay, eat, and fellowship. I think this is one of the hardest things for us to do. It's easy to look at relationship building as a method of evangelism.

Jesus did not build relationships with others because it was His evangelistic tool. He reached out to people because He had compassion on them (Matthew 9:36). Jesus genuinely cared for people and willingly spent time with them so He could know them and they could know Him. Many people had a heart change as a result (Luke 19:1-9).

We can care for people in the same way, knowing that every person has been created in God's image and is a potential kingdom disciple.

Don't say, "Oh, that's too bad." Pray. (Luke 10:9a)

Jesus told His disciples to heal the sick. Helping others to receive what they need from God through prayer is so powerful that the enemy will throw distractions at you to keep you from praying for others. These distractions include things like feelings of obligation or guilt, or bad theology that tries to explain why a person is not doing well.

We don't have to figure it out. Jesus wants to fill us with His compassion so we can love others, not condemn them, and bring the kingdom of God to bear on their situation. Ask the Holy Spirit to show you what's on God's heart for that person so you can pray for that.

When a person shares a need with you, ask, "May I pray for you right now?" Most will gladly accept. It doesn't have to be fancy. Just pray for their specific needs as the Holy Spirit leads you.

A kingdom disciple believes that "these signs will accompany those who believe" (Mark 16:17). King Jesus wants us to follow His example and heal the sick and drive out demons. It's a sign the kingdom of God is near (Matthew 10:7-8; 12:25-28). If this kind of experience is new to you, find someone who can disciple you in the power of the Holy Spirit.

As God's kingdom draws near, share with others that God has a better way (Luke 10:9b).

This fourth step is normally what is called evangelism. Positioning yourself according to Luke 10 means that you first engage your heart and your life with people, not just get them to pray the sinner's prayer. Your role is to help a person see when the kingdom of God draws near and what it means to follow the King.

We are not helping people to be good Christians. We are inviting people to repent, which means to change direction and switch kingdoms. God will not come into their kingdom; they will need to bring their kingdom into His and submit everything to King Jesus. A prayer of repentance is putting up a white flag of surrender to King Jesus and His rule. When you see the white flag go up, you can help them follow the King.

First steps to model Luke 10:

- Position yourself to bless those around you in practical ways. As you head to work ask the Lord, "How do you want me to be a blessing today?"
- Ask God how you can engage more deeply with one person at work. Think about taking them out for lunch just to find out more about them.
- Be courageous to pray for a person on the spot. Prayer is what activates kingdom advancement.

- As you see God moving in a person's life, ask the Lord how He wants you to respond. Jesus is the only way to the Father, but He does like to customize His approach for each person. As they see the kingdom of God drawing near to them, talk to them about the kingdom and help them enter personally (see page 29). Then help them find a group of people who will help them grow in the ways of King Jesus and His kingdom.

2. Keep it simple, Saints

Some people like to use the acronym K.I.S.S. as a reminder that we make things out to be more complicated than they really are. For me, K.I.S.S. stands for "Keep it simple, Saints." It's better to do something small than to do nothing at all.

Hearing testimonies of what God is doing through others can be both exciting and intimidating. Too much excitement can lead to big plans that never pan out. It's also easy to think, "I could never do that," and end up doing nothing. God just wants us to hear His voice and do what He says so He can bring His super to our natural. We will be blessed when we hear the word of God and obey it (Deuteronomy 28; Luke 11:28). This is what Jesus did, and it's what He wants us to do.

All you have to do is point to King Jesus and help others to discern His voice, get their orders from Him, and do what

He says. Then they will also be a disciple of the King and in a life-giving relationship with Him. Otherwise they end up looking to you more than they should and depend on you to hear correctly from God and pass along the information. Kingdom discipleship does not have middle management. It connects the servants right to the King.

First steps to keep it simple:

- Rest in the knowledge that God has strategically placed you where you are in the marketplace.
- Constantly remind yourself that advancing the kingdom wherever you go is your purpose in life. This will keep you on track and in the game.
- Listen to God's voice and respond to what He says.
- Disciple one person with a kingdom mindset. God wants us to disciple our families, neighborhoods, companies, entire industries, governments, presidents, and nations. But He is inviting you to start small. The size of the task may increase, but the simplicity of how to make kingdom disciples will remain the same.

3. Know your role

There is no room for role confusion on the playing field. The apostle Paul used the analogy of a body needing to know and value the role each part has (1 Corinthians 12:12-31).

The apostle Paul told the church in Ephesus to live lives worthy of the calling they had received (Ephesians 4:1-7).

To have greater clarity about your calling in the Body of Christ, let's look at three main roles in the kingdom of God and see where you fit in:

- King Jesus is the Head Coach.
- Kingdom leaders are the assistant coaches.
- Congregations are the players who minister.

King Jesus is the Head Coach

King Jesus is the Head Coach who calls the plays. Most people believe theoretically that King Jesus is in charge but are not living in that reality. Even with the best intentions, we get caught up serving a system and not growing in a relationship with Jesus. As we get caught up trying to serve all the needs out there, we can lose our focus and not even know it.

Kingdom leaders are the assistant coaches

I like to think of church leaders as kingdom coaches. On a football team, there are a number of coaches who train the players to play their positions so that the team wins. In the kingdom, the coaches are called apostles, prophets, evangelists, pastors and teachers. Ephesians 4:12-13 says that when kingdom coaches do their role, they help people:

- Know Jesus and His word
- Serve God wherever they go
- Be who God's called them to be

- Be united with others in the faith
- Grow up and become mature
- Receive all that God has for them

If you're a kingdom coach, God has given you two main responsibilities:

- Equip your players to win on the playing field.
- Unite with other coaches so the whole team wins your geographical region.

Let's take a look at each of these in greater detail.

Equipping your players: About three years ago, I was invited to speak at my local congregation. When my pastor went to the podium to introduce me, he said, "I want to ask you to forgive me for thinking that you are all here to build my ministry. The Lord showed me that I'm here to help you build your ministry."

I have been a part of a regional group in the Pass Area in Southern California for a number of years. These coaches have a heart to equip their players to win the marketplace and the world for the Head Coach, King Jesus. They outline kingdom strategy in their locker rooms, but know preaching from the front isn't enough. They understand that behind-the-scenes support and hands-on discipleship on the playing field are what really bring fruit.

Many congregations operate with 20 percent of the people doing 80 percent of the work. Running an efficient "locker room" does require dedicated volunteers and hard work. However, when kingdom coaches equip and release their people to build the kingdom wherever they go outside the church walls, energy is added inside their congregations. Everything runs better because their people are functioning better in the roles where they have passion and skill. Congregations succeed when their people succeed.

Uniting with other coaches: Each kingdom coach is responsible to equip the players (those a part of the congregation) to advance the kingdom in their geographic area. However, a kingdom coach must also unite with the other coaches on the team (other congregations) in order to win their region.

A significant change in the Pass Area region took place when the kingdom coaches made a covenant together to advance God's kingdom in this region. About five of us were meeting on Tuesday mornings to pray and seek God. The Lord told us that we weren't just supposed to teach unity, we needed to do unity.

We held hands, prayed, and decided to "do unity" so that God's kingdom would impact our region. From that point on, as the Lord would give us instructions, we started doing prophetic acts in our area.

The Lord spoke to us about repenting to the Native Americans for the sins of our forefathers. This was one of the keys God showed us to open our region. One of the leaders in the group said, God told me to do that three years ago but I didn't know what to do." Another leader was ministering to some Native Americans at the time and said he would request a meeting. Within five days of asking, we were able to meet with five different tribes in our region. About seven coaches from our region got on their knees in front of the tribes and asked for forgiveness and told them we wanted to be reconciled.

When we asked, "What can we do to be reconciled?" they told us, "Be peers with us. Work with us. We've had many meetings like this but never see the people again. We want to partner with you and work together."

Within a couple of weeks, all the congregations in our area met together to plan what our Nigerian brother called a "Wave of Worship." We chose to honor the Native Americans by allowing them to kick off the first hour of the 24-hour Wave of Worship.

The tribes led the opening processional. They walked to the front of the auditorium honoring God in their full traditional dress and culture singing, "I Have Decided to Follow Jesus." Of the two thousand people in attendance, most were in tears and God's presence was clearly tangible. All twenty-two pastors who spoke preached on advancing the kingdom of God. The next day the Native American leaders filled the pulpits of the Pass Area congregations.

From that point on we started to see the kingdom of God moving into our region. As the Pass Area coaches continue to unite and come together with their congregations to form one big team, we are discipling our region. (See the book *The Elk River Story* and testimonies from other movements around the world at www.harvestevan.org.)

Congregations are the players who minister

Christianity is more than going to good meetings. Our Head Coach has called us to be on His kingdom team. The assistant coaches equip us so that when we go to the fields of work, we are ready to help the people we work with every day.

I hear too many testimonies of people who are looking to get out of their jobs because they think God is calling them "into the ministry." If you're called to be a kingdom coach, then go for it. But if God has put you in the marketplace every day, then see your role in the marketplace as your primary ministry and advance the kingdom of God there with everything you have.

If you are in the kingdom, you are in the ministry. If you are a full-time Christian, then you are in full-time ministry. Ministry is simply serving. Those who want to be great in God's kingdom learn how to minister as servants, regardless of social class or job description (Mark 10:42-45).

I don't know what serving God in the marketplace will look like for you. But God knows and He wants to help you win. The stories I have shared are examples to show you how people like you are ministering in the marketplace.

By following some of this book's "first steps," you will begin to discover more clearly what your role looks like. Your influence may not look particularly "spiritual" on the outside. But it will have kingdom impact because of whom you are listening to and serving, not because of what you are doing.

First steps to know your role:

- When people look to you, point them to King Jesus. Encourage them to seek Him first. As they start hearing from the Lord, your role can be to help them understand what they believe God is saying.

- Conduct an internal audit regularly to make sure you are staying connected to the King and not serving a system.

- If you are a kingdom coach, set up a regular lunch appointment with one of your players who works in the marketplace. Support them in whatever way you can. Disciple them behind the scenes until they are fruitful for the kingdom in their role in the marketplace. Unite with other coaches in your region.

- Be the church, don't just go to church. It's OK to volunteer, but get out of the locker room and onto the playing field to take on the challenges of the marketplace.

4. Be a part of a team

The apostle Paul told the Corinthian church, "You are the body of Christ, and each one of you has a part in it" (1 Corinthians 12:12-27). He told them, "God has arranged the parts in the body, every one of them, just as he wanted them to be" (verse 18). Because of this, there should be no division in the body, but "Its parts should have equal concern for each other" (verse 26). Whether we like it or not, God has put everyone who comes into His kingdom on the same team. Unfortunately Christian church history has shown more division than unity. Unity is not optional if you want to move the kingdom of God forward.

Did you know that Jesus prayed for you and the team you are a part of right now? Can you believe that team includes the people who caused your church split and took half your members to start their own thing? Jesus prayed that we all would be one, just like the Father and the Son are one. He prayed that we would be brought to complete unity so that the world would know who God is. Our teamwork is actually a sign to those in the kingdom of darkness that God is with us and God loves them (John 17-20-23).

If we want to fulfill the Great Commission and disciple nations for Christ's kingdom, every part of the body has to do its part and be united under King Jesus against a common enemy, the devil. As servants of the King, we are special agents for the kingdom with special assignments that fit perfectly with how God has designed each one of us.

Kingdom disciples in the area where I live and in other areas around the world are learning to work together as one to move the darkness out of a region and let in the light. Isolated lights have a hard time kicking out big darkness. But when you combine or unite the light in every kingdom home and business in a region, it's easy to see how the kingdom of light can drive out the kingdom of darkness.

Christ has given His authority to His Church—His entire Body—not just one person or one group. We are all His body. He has given to us all that we need to unite and advance His kingdom together. Let's go for it.

First steps to be a part of a team:

- Join a marketplace network or a support group of some kind that gets you around kingdom disciples who are advancing the kingdom. You will become like those you are around.

- Ask a few people around you (a kingdom coach or another player in the marketplace) to equip and support you in your marketplace ministry.

A prayer for you

The Head Coach has taken the field and wants you to get out of the locker room and into your position. The air is fresh and the playing field is ready to be won for King Jesus.

I want to encourage you to put this book in your car or on your desk at work and pray this prayer before you begin your day:

> *Father God, open my eyes to see King Jesus and His kingdom in a new way, and see what advancing the kingdom of God in the marketplace looks like for me today. Give me courage to obey when I hear your voice. Help me to demonstrate your character and your power today. I want to be your disciple. Help*

me to keep my eyes on King Jesus so I can overcome whatever comes my way. I want to live so I can receive the prize you have for me at the end of my race. Amen.

Take Action

- Go back and choose a few of the recommended "First Steps" in this chapter to implement immediately. A great place to start is to position yourself each day in the model of Luke 10. That means each day setting yourself to be a blessing to those around you, care for them, pray for them, and then share about the kingdom with them as God directs you.

- Many of the people we pray with are hungry for more than just a quick prayer. If we see they would like more, we say, "God doesn't want to bless you just one time; He wants to come in and help you every day. Would you like that?" If they say, "Yes," I say, "Pray with me: *Lord Jesus, come in and forgive me of my sins. Fill me with your Holy Spirit. Help me each day to be who you made me to be. In Jesus; name. Amen.*" I encourage you to do the same. This is an easy way to help a person open the door of their heart to the kingdom of God.

8

You're Full of It

The Bible says that people will be full of many things in the last
days. God wants followers of Christ to be full of the Holy Spirit
and walk in the same power that raised Jesus from the dead.

L et me tell you about the most amazing city I've ever
seen. One of the most notable characteristics is how
well people work together...especially the Christians. No one
has a territorial attitude. There are no dividing walls.

The best way to describe the Christians in this city is
to use an analogy of how a profitable company functions.
People attend different congregations but see themselves like
specialized departments that are a part of the same Company.

Everyone works to improve the "employee" experience, reaches out and truly serves their "customers," and partners to grow the Company. Individual agendas do not exist. People put the Company's mission first and contribute willingly. They know there's plenty of work to do and see each other as strategic partners, not as the competition.

They assume the best about each other and work things out when problems arise. Leaders work together like fathers and mothers, caring for their children, seeking what's best for them and nurturing them according to their God-given design. They know how to serve, putting others before themselves. If one department is down, a leader from another department picks up the slack so that the Company as a whole doesn't suffer.

This city runs smoothly and people get along. People can be real with each other and are not easily offended. It's hard to get discouraged in this city! It's uncommon for much time to pass without someone giving you words of encouragement and blessing. If you do find yourself in a dark place, all you need to do is step outside your home or work place and someone is there to pray for you and care for your needs.

Jesus is so proud of this city! It's an answer to His prayer, "May they be brought to complete unity to let the world know that you sent me and have loved them even as you have loved me" (John 17:23).

Everyone in the city can feel God's love in tangible ways. Those who follow Jesus are so full of God that someone has to really want to go to hell to end up there.

Relationships and family are God's priority

The kingdom of God is a lot like this city I described. It's about relationship and family. For example, the Bible shows God as a Father, literally, "Daddy" (Romans 8:15; Galatians 4:6). Jesus is called the Bridegroom and those who follow Him His *bride* (John 3:29). Jesus is called the Head; the Church is His body (Romans 12; 1 Corinthians 12).

The kingdom of God is about a loving relationship with the King and building relationships with the citizens of that kingdom until it becomes a loving family. That family is led by a Father who cares for us even when we mess up.

God wants His family full of people who are not in it for themselves, but want the best for you and support you to be what God has designed you to be. When we live this way, we succeed and bear good fruit for God's kingdom.

Unfortunately, many people grow up in a church only to leave it for a negative reason. They seemingly walk away from God, but what they're really walking away from is a system that is full of itself rather than full of God.

The Good News is good news to those who receive it

Many years ago I was church deacon. Before one deacon's meeting I was asked to give a devotional. I had been reading two passages in the Bible and decided to share them with the guys. First I read 1 Timothy 2:4, "[God] wants all men to be saved and to come to a knowledge of the truth." Pretty straightforward, right? God loves people and doesn't want anyone to miss out on the good things He has planned.

Next I read a few verses from Psalm 103: "Praise the LORD, O my soul, and forget not all his benefits – who forgives all your sins and heals all your diseases." I finished by saying that God wants to save and heal everyone, which I thought was really good news!

One of the deacons spoke up, "Do you really believe that?" I replied, "Well, yes." He said, "How can you believe that? That's not what the Bible is saying and you shouldn't be teaching that."

As a fairly new believer, I was shocked. I was only trying to go after God and agree with His word. Now these guys were telling me I was full of it. I told God, "I thought that's what you wanted me to share because saving and healing people is on your heart. I thought they would be excited about the good news of what You want to do."

What are you full of?

The Bible says that people will be full of many things in the last days: "lovers of themselves, lovers of money, boastful, proud, abusive, disobedient to their parents, ungrateful, unholy, without love, unforgiving, slanderous, without self-control, brutal, not lovers of the good, treacherous, rash, conceited, lovers of pleasure rather than lovers of God" (2 Timothy 3:2-5). What a heavy list!

This passage says one more thing about these people: *they will have a form of godliness but deny its power.* This is what I experienced in the deacons' meeting and this is what I think is a major hindrance to us walking in God's fullness.

The apostle Paul thought being full of these things was so serious that he said to stay away from people who behaved in this way.

Religious leaders of Jesus' day weren't trying to reject God. They were trying really hard to follow Him! But they were so full of their spiritual traditions that they failed to rely upon Christ and His power (Colossians 2:8). Jesus told them that they thought so highly of their traditions that they nullified God's word (Matthew 15:6). They were "full of dead men's bones and everything unclean" (John 5:39-40; Matthew 23:27). They ended up killing the Messiah they had been waiting for.

I assume you are reading this book because you want to be full of God. That's awesome! Remember that we can be misled just as easily as those in the Bible. We need to pay attention to these words so that we deliberately fill ourselves with Jesus to "have life, and have it to the full" (John 10:10).

Repentance turns everything around

What does someone full of God look like? Look at the life of Jesus. Jesus is the standard and the Bible says that we all have fallen short of that standard (Romans 3:23). That's why Jesus' first sermon was a call to repent (Matthew 4:17; Mark 1:14-15).

Jesus told people to repent of the wrong thinking that had separated them from God. Jesus came to lead us into new kingdom thinking, so He said, "Repent," so we could get on the right path.

There are two parts to the word *repent*:

- **Re** = The first part of repentance is to turn from the way you are going. Isaiah 55:7 says, "Let the wicked forsake his way and the evil man his thoughts. Let him turn to the Lord, and he will have mercy on him, and to our God, for he will freely pardon." Until we are willing to forsake our own way, God's mercy is not available for us. God can only pardon those who admit their wrong and are willing to make a change.

- **Pent** = The second part of repentance is to agree that God's ways are higher than ours. Isaiah 55:9 says, "As the heavens are higher than the earth, so are my ways higher than your ways and my thoughts than your thoughts." Think of the word penthouse. Repentance is seeing God's desire to move us to a higher place in His house and following Him to that place.

Repentance is changing your mind to agree with God. Repentance feels like a dirty word because none of us likes to be wrong. A colonoscopy is a very unpleasant procedure, but it's effective in showing your doctor possible problems.

I think Christians needs a kingdomoscopy—that's where you allow God to stick His light into your life and show you all the crud He wants to clean out. God doesn't show you the crud to make you feel bad. He shows it to you so you ask for a spiritual enema to flush out the waste in your life.

Those who are hungry will be filled

It's easy to be full of stuff that's of no use to God. Because we fill ourselves with these things, we have no idea how empty we really are. It's like filling your stomach with junk food. Your stomach is full so you don't feel hungry, but your health is poor because what you're eating is unhealthy.

Jesus wants us to see our condition so we ask for His help. He said, "It is not the healthy who need a doctor, but the sick. For I have not come to call the righteous, but sinners" (Matthew 9:12-13). Basically He's saying, "Until you know you have a problem, you're probably not going to reach out to me in a significant way." Jesus wants us hungry and thirsty for His righteousness because He knows those are the ones who will be filled (Matthew 5:6; 6:33).

We can be just like Jesus

God expects nothing less than we be just like Jesus. This isn't supposed to be depressing; it's exciting! Through the Holy Spirit we can be who Jesus was on the inside and do what He did on the outside. The way to accomplish this is to stay constantly connected to the Father like Jesus was.

Many people want the benefits of being a part of God's kingdom, but fewer want to nurture a relation-ship with the King of that kingdom and be accountable to His wishes.

How to mature into a kingdom citizen and walk in His power

Our faith is more than going to church and trying hard to be a good person for God. Jesus sent His Spirit to help us mature as citizens in His kingdom and use the keys of the kingdom each day on earth to prepare ourselves and others for His return (Hebrews 6:1-3).

Can you imagine what an adult would look like with a baby's body except a mature head, hands, and feet? We would call that person deformed. That's how many of us end up spiritually. We stuff our heads with knowledge and stay busy going places and doing things but fail to develop in other areas just as important to God. I've seen so many people chewed up because they've tried to do God's work through their own ambition and power. They get spun real hard one or two times and are down for the count. They continue to drift or are still recovering today.

In 1915, AAA was the first company to offer assistance to stranded motorists. God has his own triple A roadside assistance for the journey He has for you. His program will help you stay on the right road and get to your destination on time. It'll also help you mature as a kingdom citizen and release God's presence in your city.

God's three A's are:

Abide: To stay connected to God we must remain in His presence. God's presence helps us to see things like He does and remain in a loving relationship with the Father and with His family. Once we see, then we can agree.

Agree: We must stop depending on our own understanding, see life from God's perspective, and align ourselves with His will. Once we agree, then we need to act.

Act: A prophetic act is hearing God's voice and acting on it. Faith without works is dead. Those who love God will naturally respond to God by giving themselves passionately to the cause of the kingdom. This produces God's powerful hope in our lives and in the lives of others around us.

Abiding, agreeing, and acting are one package. Think of it like ingredients in a soup. The ingredients are mixed together to make something greater than any one of its parts. You can't separate them in any way without having negative effects.

In the next three chapters, we're going to look at these powerful three ingredients: *abiding* in God, *agreeing* with God, and then *acting* by giving ourselves to the cause of His kingdom. Even though we'll talk about them in different chapters, remember that they must be mixed together in equal parts to bear the fruit God has for you in His kingdom.

Take Action

- What do your daily actions demonstrate that you are the most full of?

- If you are finding yourself full of things you do not want, consider going on a fast. Temporarily or permanently abstain from those things.

- What is one way you can abide, agree, and act this week?

- Whatever you're full of will either energize your life in God or compete against it. God is willing to fill us with His Spirit if we will ask (Luke 11:13; Matthew 7:11). Ask right now: *God, I don't want to be full of myself. I want to be full of You and walk in the same power that raised Jesus from the dead. Clean me out and make me hungry for Your righteousness. Fill me afresh with Your Holy Spirit.*

Abiding in God

To stay connected to God we must remain in His presence.
God's presence helps us to see things like He does and remain
in a loving relationship with the Father and with His family.

We enter this world through birth by our earthly mothers. Jesus said that no one can see the kingdom of God unless they are born a second time by the Spirit. This is how we make our initial connection with God. God doesn't expect that we come into His family and then go off to try to make things happen on our own. He wants us to remain connected to Him all the time and follow Him. That way we'll end up where He wants us to be.

God doesn't want us to run on batteries

When Jesus was talking to His disciples about the days before His return, He told a story of ten virgins who took their lamps out to meet a Bridegroom (a picture of Himself). Five had extra oil; five did not. The oil can represent our connection to the life of the Holy Spirit.

Because they had to wait longer than expected, the foolish virgins ran out of batteries and had to run to the store to get new ones. While they were gone, He showed up. When they returned from the store, they asked the Bridegroom to open the door and let them in. His response was, "I don't know you" (Matthew 25:1-12).

God doesn't expect us to run on batteries. He wants us to stay plugged into Him so that we get to know Him and always have what we need. Our connection to God is what allows us to have a fruitful life and walk in hope no matter what our circumstances are.

Seek first the Source, not His resources

It's easy to seek God to get our needs met and not seek to know God Himself. In the same way a spouse should be a partner and friend, God is our partner and friend, not just someone who serves our needs.

A key Scripture that God gave to me early in my business was Matthew 6:33, "But seek first his kingdom and his righteousness, and all these things will be given to you as well." There was a liquor store near my business and people would gather outside. When I had slow times at work, I used to walk to the store thinking, "Hey, I'm going to seek first the kingdom and see who needs prayer."

Whenever I would go to the liquor store to bring the kingdom of God to the people standing outside, within a short time my lead manager would come out and say, "Dick we have business. You need to order some supplies." This happened numerous times. The enemy may have been holding up the work or God may have been blessing me for advancing His kingdom, maybe both. Either way, we got work whenever I chose to seek first the kingdom of God.

God's presence changed the factory

When communism fell in Albania in the early 1990s, we were some of the first people to bring the gospel into Albania. During our stay, our guide and translator said, "I know a woman who runs a factory. Could we go see her?"

We talked to the Muslim woman in charge and told her that we'd like to bless and encourage the workers. She was adamant that she didn't want us to do that. We asked, "Can we pray a blessing for you?" She agreed. While we were praying, she seemed to go to sleep standing up for about five minutes. The translator asked her, "Are you OK? Where have you been?" She opened her eyes and said, "I was with God," and then gave us the OK to pray for the workers and bless them.

We spent the next four days in that factory praying for five floors containing 800 workers. The woman even gave us a room to use. We led many to the Lord and brought the kingdom of God into the factory.

In over twenty subsequent trips, we ministered to hundreds of business people in Albania. We saw God open many doors and perform signs and wonders to advance His kingdom in the marketplace. It all started when one woman entered into God's presence.

God's presence unlocks understanding

A few years ago I was sitting on the front deck at a cabin with my friends Josh and Ken. Josh asked Ken if he would take him into the third heaven. I was amused by Josh's request and a bit skeptical. Ken said, "Sure, when?" Josh replied, "Right now!" Then Ken reminded us that the only way we enter in is by faith.

I don't know if we were in the third heaven, but God's presence was with us in a powerful way. Two hours later, it didn't seem like time had passed. We understood things we had not understood previously. We saw things from God's point of view. At times it was like combinations were spinning and locks were opening. We had been in God's presence.

God designed us for relationship and the only way to get to know God is by being with Him. We can read, hear, think, and talk about God and still not connect with God. Being in God's presence gives us the opportunity to see things from His point of view and be changed through the encounter. God's presence exposes our wrong thinking so we can repent and get our thoughts aligned with His.

Lean on God's perspective, not your own

Proverbs 3:5-6 says that we should not depend on our own understanding. Instead, we should know God's heart in all our ways. When we do this, God directs us in His paths. Psalm 23:3 says that God leads us in paths of righteousness for *His* name's sake. Jesus came to establish *His* government, not fix everyone else's. Our role is to cooperate with God to see His will done on earth as it is in heaven.

Leaning on your own understanding is like walking on thin ice. The surface looks smooth and solid, but when you put your full weight on it, you fall through. This is why God tells us not to lean on something as fickle as our own understanding. This is also why God wants you to spend time in His presence so you come to know Him and His ways.

God's presence can knock you off your horse

The apostle Paul's first encounter with God was dramatic. He was going about his own business when he rode into God's presence and got knocked off his horse. One way to look at it is that the light of Jesus knocked the hell (all the junk) out of Paul. Paul's turnaround was so significant that he turned from being the chief persecutor of Christians to being the Christian at the top of the list to be persecuted!

We need to let God's light knock the hell out of us too so we can receive all that heaven has to offer. I've often wondered why sometimes people fall down when they get prayed for. Could it be that they are getting knocked off their horse and God is taking the hell out of them? Humility and sanctification are a process, so this is needed for Christians too! Those who allow God to do this are the ones who in turn receive power to release God's awesome presence in their cities.

Remaining in God takes discipline

Just after Paul's conversion, we don't hear much from him for about 14 years. What was going on? Paul wasn't lacking in zeal. As a Pharisee, Paul had superior knowledge of the Scriptures. He didn't need to go to college to take Torah classes. I believe God used this time to mature Paul. We see this in most of the major characters in the Bible. Learning to remain in God takes time. God uses time to instill discipline in us so we stay connected and cooperate with Him.

Psalm 1:3 is a good picture of what life is like when we stay connected to God, just like Jesus did. The Bible says that blessed are those who don't listen to the clutter of the world but delight in keeping God's word on their mind. They are like a tree planted by streams of water that bears fruit in its season. This tree doesn't wither and prospers in everything. When we stay rooted in God, we mature and grow as He has designed, just like a tree grows and bears fruit as it stays firmly rooted in the ground.

Staying connected and remaining in God's presence help us to *see* things like He does and remain in a loving relationship with the Father and with His family. Once we *see*, then we can *agree*, which is what we will talk about in the next chapter.

Take Action

- Have you ever seen better results when you seek to know God Himself and not just seeking to get your needs met?
- What does seeking God's kingdom first look like for you?
- Remaining "planted" in God is the only way we get what we need to prosper in what God has for us. Tell God that you're not going to pull out when you feel tempted to disconnect or quit. Pray with me: *God, thank you for the hard things I've faced in my life. They've led me to You. Come into the difficult situation I'm in right now and walk with me through it. I know You're committed to me. I want to stay connected to You no matter what. Work in me what's pleasing in Your sight so my life honors You. Amen.*

CHAPTER

10

Agreeing with God

———◦———

Godly agreement releases God's power and blessing.
We must stop depending on our own understanding, see life
from God's perspective, and align ourselves with His will.

Joshua had just led all of Israel across the Jordan River to
stage their first battle for the Promised Land. Joshua 5:13-
15 says:

> Now when Joshua was near Jericho, he looked up
> and saw a man standing in front of him with a
> drawn sword in his hand. Joshua went up to him
> and asked, "Are you for us or for our enemies?"
>
> "Neither," he replied, "but as commander of the
> army of the LORD I have now come." Then

Joshua fell facedown to the ground in reverence, and asked him, "What message does my Lord have for his servant?"

The commander of the LORD's army replied, "Take off your sandals, for the place where you are standing is holy." And Joshua did so.

I love this story. You'd think that the commander of the Lord's army would have said, "Hey Josh, I'm on your side and have got you covered." Instead he says, "I'm not on your side. I'm on God's side and it would be a good idea if you made sure you are on God's side too!"

Don't you think our lives in God's family would be much easier if we all took this approach? There is so much competition and disconnectedness between congregations. God wants us to have a mindset of family and relationship. God isn't for anyone's side. He's for His own side. So why don't we learn to discern together what God wants, agree, and move forward together. I think we'd see walls like Jericho come down around us regularly.

Agreement with perseverance brings miracles

A friend of mine named David was legally blind. He could not see anything at a distance and to read he had to put the book right in front of his face.

David went with me on my first trip to Mongolia in 1990. I remember him saying constantly, "God's going to heal me." For years he agreed with God for his healing. At the time I would chuckle because it was easy to think, "Oh God, how is that ever going to happen." This went on for years.

How many people do we know who say the same thing for years, with no results. David continued to contend for what God had spoken to him despite his circumstances and in the midst of everyone else's unbelief.

About a year ago I got a picture in the mail of David sitting in a sports car. He now has his driver's license and is able to see clearly.

I wonder who was really blind. I think it was me. It's easy to see and agree with circumstances around us and think it must be God's will. But when we agree with what God says in the midst of whatever we're facing, we get to see miracles happen. In Five Yards and a Cloud of Dust, I talk more about how to persevere until you see God break through into your situation.

Use your energy to trust God

Did you know that it takes the same amount of energy to trust God as it does to live in unbelief? When I owned my manufacturing business, a company asked me to create a product for them. After running production for a few days, the product looked great. But because the sizing wasn't right, I had to fix the problem and rerun production. It wasn't any harder to make the product the right way the second time than it was to make it the wrong way the first time. The key is to get things right at the beginning.

You're going to put out energy whatever you do, whether you agree or disagree with God. So why not agree with God and His Word the first time and come out with a life that really works.

Agree with God about your problem and His solution

Melissa was only eighteen when she got into a car accident that stretched her spinal cord. She had reached over to her sister in the passenger's seat to brace her from the impact and ended up with more than two years of painful disability in a wheelchair.

A friend told me about this girl and asked if I would go and pray for her. On the way there the Lord said to me, "Just help her to agree with My word." When I arrived I explained, "Here's the deal. I can pray tender prayers for you and say some encouraging words. But God showed me that 'if two of you on earth agree about anything you ask for, it will be done for you by your Father in heaven' (Matthew 18:19). Let's go with what Jesus said and also with what the Bible says in Isaiah 53:5 and 1 Peter 2:24:

> 'But he was pierced for our transgressions, he was crushed for our iniquities; the punishment that brought us peace was upon him, and by his wounds we are healed.'

> 'He himself bore our sins in his body on the tree, so that we might die to sins and live for righteousness; by his wounds you have been healed.'

"You are probably full of questions and hurt. We can try to figure out what you've been going through these two years or we can just agree together on the truth of God's word."

So we prayed and agreed with God about His word. The Lord also prompted me to share with her that the pain meant she was healing. As I left she gave me permission to call and check up on her.

The next week she got worse. Someone told me, "I hear you went to pray for that girl and they had to take her to the hospital." It was like the enemy was saying, "You think those little prayers of agreement are going to change my plans for her? I'm going to make her suffer more." The pain did get worse and continued. I would call Melissa and there would be no change. I would ask the Lord, "What is happening? What about your word?" The enemy would reply, "What word?" I would respond, "The word of the Lord is true and you have to obey."

The next time I talked to my friends they said, "Did you hear? She's healed." I talked with Melissa after this and she said, "On August 30, 2007, all the pain went away."

Now Melissa is comforting others with the same comfort that God gave to her (see 2 Corinthians 1:4).

What does it mean to agree with God?

Agreeing with God is a lot like the Whac-A-Mole kids' game where moles pop up through a hole and the player uses a mallet to knock them down. When the enemy pops things up in your life, you have to take thoughts captive and pop them with the truth of God's word and then put them under the obedience of Christ.

I've already shared how my company was buried in debt and I had no way to get out. As I prayed, God spoke to me to repent of debt. I agreed with God about my problem and repented.

The next day God spoke to me to give $400 to a man when I only had $800 in my checking account and payroll was due. Even though it seemed very foolish, I wrote the check. I also told my employees that I was turning the company over to God and asked them to forgive me for running the company into the ground. Everyone was sure I had lost it. Actually it was just the start of me getting it.

The change didn't come because God made me smarter. I couldn't work any harder. I couldn't do anything to earn it or make the situation change. All I could do was agree with God that I had sinned by getting into debt, repent, and obey what God was saying.

God showed me that repentance is agreeing that I was wrong and He was right. God showed me that repentance means turning around and seeing my life from God's perspective. Agreement has feet. Agreeing with God produces a response of some kind, because "faith by itself, if it is not accompanied by action, is dead" (James 2:17).

Good fruit came from my agreement with God: I made payroll that month, I didn't get myself into debt when things began to look up, and within a year and a half, my business was completely out of debt. Many of my employees came to the Lord after I repented of debt and invited Christ's kingdom into my business.

The word of God is your best weapon

The weapon that God has given us to fight our battles is His word. The word of God is our sword (Ephesians 6:17). If you do not agree with what God has given you to fight with, then how effective are you in fighting the enemy?

For example, Psalm 103:3-5 tells us not to forget God's benefits: He "forgives all your sins and heals all your diseases, [He] redeems your life from the pit and crowns you with love and compassion, [He] satisfies your desires with good things so that your youth is renewed like the eagle's." If we do not agree that God forgives ALL and heals ALL, then we are at odds with the word of God.

When bad things happen and we question God's love, we are at odds with His word. When we have been patiently waiting for our desires to be fulfilled and get angry at God for taking such a long time, we are not agreeing with the word of God. An untrustworthy weapon is useless, and that is what we make the word of God when we don't agree with it.

The only offensive weapon we have is "the sword of the Spirit, which is the word of God" (Ephesians 6:17). Paul told the Ephesians "Put on the full armor of God, so that when the day of evil comes, you may be able to stand your ground, and after you have done everything, to stand" (6:13).

We stand against the lies of the enemy (that which doesn't agree with God's word) using our shield of faith. Our shield quenches these lies so we can agree with God's word and declare truth.

Bad circumstances may cloud God's word, but they do not nullify it. Agreeing with God's word is not foolish or ignorant; it's putting our trust in what is stable and unchangeable. When circumstances tempt us to question if God's word is true, we need to agree with God and what He has said, use the word of God against the enemy, and contend for what God has said as long as it takes to see it happen.

During the time of difficulty with my business, the Holy Spirit spoke to me: "Owe nothing to anyone except to love one another" (Romans 13:8, NASB). I agreed with God and I have stayed out of debt since that time. When opposition came I told the enemy, "The Lord told me to owe nothing to anyone except to love one another." This word was the sword I used to fight the enemy.

The word of God has serious knockdown power against the enemy. The Holy Spirit put power in the word; if you have the word, you have power. If you don't have the word, the enemy will take you out. Your chances increase dramatically when you agree with God, respond to what He says, and refuse to make excuses for what may look like a loss. When things aren't looking good, God wants you to focus on His trustworthy character and keep moving forward.

You don't need to understand, just agree

You don't need to *understand* the situation or all that God is saying, you just need to *agree* with God. Friends will tell you, "That's not what the word of God really means." Stay true to what God spoke to you. The first step to agreeing with God is to know if you believe that the word of God—*all* of God's word—is true.

The only way the word of God is a reliable weapon is if you agree with it consistently and interpret life by what it says. Most people interpret God's word by their circumstances. "I'm sick and not getting better, so God must not want me to be healed" or "I've done many bad things and don't feel God will forgive me." Don't let your circumstances determine if God's word is true. When we do that, it's like putting on a pair of dirty glasses that distort what we can see. God wants to correct our vision by looking through the lens of His word and believe it is true regardless of external circumstances.

How to agree with the Holy Spirit in prayer

Have you ever felt you should pray for someone? You think, "Is this me or God?" All you have to say is, "Holy Spirit, I agree with you that this person needs You. Do you want me to pray? If so, help me love them like you do and give me courage in Jesus' name." When you pray for them, simply ask, "Would you agree with me and God for what you need?" Then thank God for His provision and say whatever else God tells you.

God wants us to pray from a place of the finished work of Jesus. People often pray like this: "Jesus, we need Your help, we need You to show up, please!" God wants us to pray, "Jesus, thank You for Your healing power. We agree with Your finished work and that by Your stripes we are healed. Your word is true and we agree with Your plans in this person's life."

God will answer prayer when we agree with Him. John 15:7-8 says, "If you abide in Me, and My words abide in you, ask whatever you wish, and it will be done for you. My Father is glorified by this, that you bear much fruit, and so prove to be My disciples." Jesus is saying, "When you and My words are in complete agreement, ask and you will receive. There's more. This isn't just about you getting your prayers answered. My Father is glorified when good things happen and you prove that you're really my disciples."

Some people get nervous when they hear someone talk about this verse. It's usually because they've asked and didn't receive the way they expected. Or they think people will just ask for their own selfish gain. Neither change that this is what God's word says and He wants you to believe it.

A few weeks ago I was returning from the Philippines with my friend, Larry. We were waiting to get on the plane and heard the gate agent say, "There will be a half-hour delay." They began to pull off people who had already boarded the plane. I said to Larry, "We need to agree together that we're going to leave on time." So we prayed together.

Then they made another announcement, "It's going to be another hour." I said to Larry, "We just agreed together so they don't have much time to get us on the plane." Within three minutes, they announced, "We're loading the plane. We fixed the problem." We were first in line, got on the plane, and the plane left on time. I shared with a guy on the plane that we prayed to leave on time. "Prayer must work," he replied, and I had a chance to talk to him about God.

Those who agree will succeed

A few years ago we were invited to be a part of the one-hundred-year celebration of a significant Church history event, which included a huge conference and a number of workshops for about one hundred thousand people.

We were asked by the organizers to provide an opportunity for people to go to the businesses in the downtown area and pray for them. We passed out thousands of invitations to let people know about this opportunity.

The first day fifteen people showed up. We went out each day and about the same fifteen came with us each time. Our little group ended up praying for over two thousand people, about seven hundred businesses, and led over two hundred people to the Lord. People were very receptive and the Holy Spirit was moving in the city. Unfortunately, the church was inside a building, even though there was a concentration of energy that could have been used to affect the city in a powerful way.

I know this sounds critical. I'm not saying that if the conference participants followed our group we would have saved the city. But I do think that if we would follow Christ and the leading of the Holy Spirit *corporately* as the body of Christ, our largest, most powerful cities could be reached in a very short time.

A *few* of us went out, did a *little* bit, and had an impact on *thousands* of people. It doesn't take many people to accomplish great things for God's kingdom. It does take agreement with God and with each other to see the kingdom of God come to our work places and cities.

Jesus' prayer was for real and it's for now:

> "Your kingdom come, Your will be done on earth
> as it is in heaven" (Matthew 6:10).

There is no shortage of laborers. We're just short on agreement and a willingness to do whatever it takes to reach our cities for Christ.

Agreement with God keeps the hell out of us

I shared before that being in God's presence changes our minds and takes the venom out of us. It also produces a desire to get into alignment with God and His plan for our lives.

Agreeing with God keeps the evil out and gives us comfort that we're not trying to make things happen on our own. We are simply agreeing with Him and following King Jesus.

Agreement is full cooperation with God

Imagine being a teenage girl who has an angel show up one day to say, "You're going to have a baby, and by the way, the baby is going to be the Son of God." When Mary asked how it was going to happen, the angel's answer wasn't much more comforting. Mary was about to conceive a baby in a way no woman in history had experienced. Mary's response to this mysterious challenge was, "I am the Lord's servant. May it be to me as you have said" (Luke 1:38).

When Joseph found out Mary was pregnant, he was going to do the honorable thing and divorce her quietly. Then an angel appeared to him in a dream and explained what was going on. Both Mary and Joseph chose to agree with God and did what they were told to do. Their agreement set the stage for the birth of the Messiah.

This same attitude will bring Jesus into whatever situation you are in. Whatever God says, respond, "OK, I agree with what You say and will cooperate."

When you agree, miracles happen

Whenever you see success in the Bible, someone was agreeing with God.

- Noah agreed with God that a flood was coming even though no one had seen rain before.
- Abraham agreed with God that he would have a son at a very old age and his descendants would be as numerous as the sands of the sea.

- Moses agreed with God that lifting up his staff at the Red Sea would create a path for a million people to cross over.
- Joshua and Caleb agreed with God and entered into the Promised Land at an old age when all of their peers did not.
- Deborah agreed with God that Israel would defeat an opposing king even though someone else was supposed to be the leader.
- Gideon agreed with God that an army of 300 could defeat massive armies rallied against him.
- David agreed with God that Goliath was not too big and he was not too small.
- Nehemiah agreed with God that He wanted to rebuild His temple and that it would happen more quickly than anyone could have predicted.
- Jesus agreed with His Father in every word and action and saved the world from sin and death.
- Multitudes agreed with Jesus and were healed.
- The disciples and apostles agreed with the Holy Spirit and performed many miracles in the name of Jesus.
- For two thousand years, followers of Jesus around the world have chosen to agree with God and have accomplished amazing things for His kingdom.

Agreement has feet

Agreement always means responding to God in some way. Agreement is not passive mental agreement. It is full of faith and proactive. Noah started building an ark. Moses lifted up his staff. David went to the brook to pick up some stones. Joseph married Mary. These people did not just nod their heads in token agreement. This was faith at its premium and there was a lot to lose if God didn't come through.

The key to remember is this: when the Lord gives you a word, you don't have to understand; just agree and act on that agreement to see things begin to happen in your life. Our mind always wants to get in the way of agreeing with God. This is why the Bible talks about the need to renew our minds.

A renewed mind is in 100 percent agreement with God

A totally renewed mind is in *total* agreement with God and His word. In heaven, when we receive full understanding, we will completely agree with God. God is asking us *before* we get to heaven, based on His word, to believe in Him with the same amount of conviction as if we were in heaven already.

Real agreement is wholehearted. *Wholehearted* means our souls (our mind, will, and emotions) are in complete submission to the Spirit of the Lord. Wholeheartedness is loving God by believing Him with *all* your heart, *all* your mind, and with *all* your soul. We can't do anything more than agree with God. God has done through Jesus Christ all that He is going to do. It's a finished work and our job is to agree with God and act on it. We don't have to talk God into something He's already done.

Millions of people have believed 1 John 1:9 and have come to faith in Jesus: "If we confess our sins, he is faithful and just and will forgive us our sins and purify us from all unrighteousness." We agree with God for our salvation. We need to take the same kind of faith and apply it to the rest of our lives.

It's easy to think we agree with God, but our actions often don't show it. Conceptually we believe in the existence of God but misapply His word in our daily lives. May I ask you a question that usually uncovers the degree to which you believe God's word? Here it is: *Is disease and sickness good or bad?*

The Bible states that the curse and its symptoms (sin, disease, sickness, death) are the result of Adam and Eve's sin in the Garden of Eden. Jesus took the entire curse upon Himself so we could live life on earth just like it is in heaven (Genesis 3; Psalm 103; Isaiah 53; Galatians 3; Matthew 6:10). And heaven isn't hindered by the curse in any way.

The Bible warns us not to call what is evil "good" and what is good "evil" (Isaiah 5:20). We call bad "good" when we attribute the works of the devil to God. Remember, Jesus came to destroy the works of the devil (1 John 3:8). God is the one who can turn the things the enemy meant for evil to good. The Bible makes a clear distinction: God is good, the devil is bad (James 1:13-18); Jesus came to give abundant life, and the goal of the devil is always to steal, kill, and destroy (John 10:10). We can believe in God and His word. If you're going to doubt, doubt your doubt, but have faith in God.

God asks us to renew our minds with what the word of God says, not with what life experience has taught us. Even though bad things happen, God wants us to believe Him no matter how it looks and know He'll work things out for our good (Romans 8:28).

The process looks like this: the Holy Spirit speaks something to us, it lines up with the Bible, we agree, and we act. When we see things that are not of God and they have place in our lives, we renounce them. We take off the bad lies and put on the good truth of the Bible.

That's how our minds get renewed. A renewed mind is in total agreement with God. When I don't know what to do, I just need to find out what God's word says and hear His voice. I don't have to strive and struggle, I just agree and contend in faith until the breakthrough happens.

Agreement with God closes the circuit and brings the power

When you agree with God, it's like flipping a power switch. The circuit closes and allows the power to flow. Renewing the mind keeps you in the circuit of power. The word of God keeps you in alignment with what keeps the power flowing.

Doubt breaks the circuit. When the circuit gets loaded with too much doubt, it breaks and the power shuts off.

Many people have broken circuits. Renewing the mind also makes the circuit stronger so that it doesn't pop.

Like I shared in the chapter "Five Yards and a Cloud of Dust," you have to contend. You can't change your mind tomorrow when you don't see the results you were hoping for. Life isn't like a fast-food drive-through. It takes perseverance to see the breakthrough. Your soul is the hinge that determines if the circuit is closed and the power of God is flowing in your life.

Jesus said, "If a kingdom is divided against itself, that kingdom cannot stand. If a house is divided against itself, that house cannot stand" (Mark 3:24-25). An open circuit is like a divided house. This type of house does not have power and will not stand. However, the opposite of what Jesus said is also true: a house united—in agreement—does stand.

Agreement with God helps us get along and get the job done

Agreement with God has power over disagreement. Have you ever been in a situation where no one can agree? It's so frustrating. What if when disagreement arises, the group could agree that the one thing they all want is what God wants. When a group of people do that, there's great power to hear from God and release the Father to have His way in His family.

Jesus said that "if two of you on earth agree about anything you ask for, it will be done for you by my Father in heaven. For where two or three come together in my name, there am I with them" (Matthew 18:19-20). I've said that God's presence helps us to agree. Jesus also says here that when we agree, God's presence is with us. So it works both ways.

We know agreement is powerful. Those who gathered to build the tower of Babel showed unprecedented agreement, so much so that God said that nothing would be impossible for them (Genesis 11:6). Unfortunately, their agreement was not in alignment with God's will.

When our agreement is in alignment with God's will, groups can move forward without the venom of individual agendas. People can say, "We're good with what God wants to do. Let's rest in that and move forward together." Everyone gets to see God move and does not have to labor to get the work done. Everyone is at rest and follows God as He leads and drives His own agenda.

We were recently with about two hundred students at Stout University in Wisconsin. At the end of our time together I asked if I could say the closing prayer. I said, "The Lord would like to be invited into Stout U. If we agree together and invite God's presence onto this campus, I believe God will be here, in your classrooms, and in your lives in a more significant way." I had them all pray with me, "Lord Jesus, we agree with You and what You want for Stout University. We invite You to come and be with us."

I talked to one of the students later who said that from that meeting, things began to change at the school. We've led groups in prayers like this and always see a significant change when wills surrender to His will and agree with His plan.

The struggle to get along and get anything done can be so stressful sometimes. Jesus wants to reveal the Father's heart to us so we can learn from Him and find rest instead of strife. Jesus' invitation is to "Come to me, all you who are weary and burdened, and I will give you rest. Take my yoke upon you and learn from me, for I am gentle and humble in heart, and you will find rest for your souls. For my yoke is easy and my burden is light" (Matthew 11:28-30). This is a much better way to live!

Your soul is the hinge

The soul is made up of your mind, will, and emotions. Your soul is the "hinge" that determines the decisions you make. When your soul takes sides with your flesh, you move in the flesh. When your soul takes sides with the Holy Spirit in your spirit, you move with the Spirit.

This is how decisions are made. You receive input of some kind. Your soul interprets this information (what you think about it—your mind, and how you feel about it—your emotions). If your mind is renewed, your soul will interpret the input through God's word and you will have strength in your will to choose to follow the Spirit. If you have not trained your soul to spin the input based on the word of God, your soul (your will) will go the direction of your flesh.

Picture this struggle as a tug of war. The Spirit is on one side, the enemy on the other, and your soul is in the middle.

Whichever side your soul decides to join and pull for wins. It takes a conscious choice of your mind and will to move to the side of the Spirit and pull in that direction. Agreeing with your flesh, or even sympathizing with your flesh and making no choice at all, heads you in the direction of self—your flesh. God asks you to make a passionate decision to agree with His word and focus your strength there. Pull!

Before Jesus began His public ministry, the Holy Spirit led Him into the desert to be tempted by the devil. Each of the temptations was an appeal to Jesus' flesh. The enemy tried to get Jesus' soul to follow His flesh. Jesus defeated each temptation by agreeing with the word of God, declaring it, and choosing to follow the Spirit instead of His flesh.

Jesus' soul was in complete submission to the Spirit His entire life. The Bible says that He was in 100 percent agreement with His Father all the time. He saw the Father doing and He did the same (John 5:19). Jesus' will always chose His Father's side and never the flesh (John 5:30). Even the words Jesus spoke were in response to His Father (John 14:10). This is a picture of complete agreement.

A soul at rest will pass the test

In the Garden of Gethsemane, just before He was betrayed and arrested, Jesus told His disciples, "My soul is overwhelmed with sorrow to the point of death" (Matthew 26:38). But even then He said to His Father, "Not as I will, but as You will" (Matthew 26:39). His soul was so overwhelmed that it wanted to side with the flesh, but His soul sided with the Spirit and His flesh came alongside and was crucified. His soul lined up with the Holy Spirit and pulled His flesh in the right direction.

Jesus knew that He could have called upon seventy-two thousand angels at any time (Matthew 26:53). But even under the greatest pressure any human has ever experienced, His soul was at rest because He agreed with the will of His Father.

You can live this way this too. Jesus came to save your soul. He saved you by passionately yielding His mind, will, and emotions over to God. He asks you to do the same. God knows it's a battle.

The apostle Paul himself wrote about this struggle to the church in Rome, "For what I do is not the good I want to do; no, the evil I do not want to do—this I keep on doing" (Romans 7:19).

Read Psalm 42-43. The writer says that his soul is downcast and distressed. But a number of times he directs his soul to "put your hope in God." God will also give you strength and courage to do this.

Hebrews 5:7 describes how Jesus "offered up prayers and petitions with loud cries and tears to the one who could save him from death." God heard His prayers because Jesus submitted to the Father's will instead of His own.

Jesus experienced what it was like to obey when obeying meant suffering. Because of Jesus' choice to deny Himself and trust His Father, He became the giver of eternal salvation to those who would obey Him in the same way.

Are we willing to sacrifice whatever it takes so that others may be saved? If we're not full of God, our spirit may be willing, but our flesh says, "No!" If we learn to surrender to what the Lord wants to do, nothing is impossible.

When you agree with God about whatever situation you're in and your soul comes into alignment with the Spirit, the flesh doesn't have a chance. It will follow. When you're in agreement with God, you're in the majority and the majority wins!

Leave your default and side with God

Remember that your human default will always go the way of the flesh until you train yourself to go the way of the Spirit. A conscious choice of your will to go against your natural default is necessary to make progress. This is why it's so important to agree with God's word first because it provides the strength and hope you need to go against what seems right to the flesh. The Bible says, "There is a way that appears to be right, but in the end it leads to death" (Proverbs 14:12; 21:2). The way of the flesh always ends in death. The Bible also says that "the mind of sinful man is death, but the mind controlled by the Spirit is life and peace" (Romans 8:6).

Paul says that we need to actively forget what is behind and pursue what is ahead. Any person who wants to follow Jesus is asked to do this. Matthew left his tax booth (Matthew 9:9); Peter and John left their nets (Matthew 4:19-20); Jesus asked a rich young ruler to leave his riches, but sadly, his kingdom was more valuable to him than the kingdom of

God (Mark 10:7-31). When we are born again and make Jesus the Lord of our lives, we are not asking God to come into our lives. We are actually forsaking our lives and coming into *His* kingdom, coming into *His* life.

Agree first and emotions will follow

Many people don't make good decisions when things are tough because "I don't feel like it." The flesh will never feel like denying itself what it wants, so we can't look to our feelings for direction. Our soul dictates to our emotions. If our soul is at rest with God, then our emotions will be at rest with God. If the mind is not renewed, it can feed the soul bad information, which fires up the feelings and the flesh. A transformed mind agrees with the Word of God. When it feeds information to the soul, it feeds right information. Then the soul sides with the Spirit, which can lead the feelings and flesh in God's ways.

Agreement is good for you

Judges 13-16 tells the story of Samson. Samson had incredible favor of God on his life and led the nation of Israel for 20 years. He started out well, but over time took God's direction less and less seriously. You could say that he stopped agreeing with God's word. This led to being seduced and deceived by a woman, getting his eyes gouged out, losing his dignity and his life. At the end, he came back into agreement with God, but was so beat up by then he died with his enemies.

Many people walk Samson's path. They may start out agreeing with God, but lose their way, get themselves into bad situations, get beat up, lose their strength and the vision God designed them to have. Don't you think it is to our advantage to agree with God and not have to go through all the trouble that we bring on ourselves? Life is hard no matter what. Why not make it better by living in agreement with God so you have His favor and His support.

You're supposed to be full of it—full of Him!

Besides Joshua, Caleb was the only other Israelite who came out of Egypt *and* entered the Promised Land. This is what God said of Caleb: "But because my servant Caleb has a different spirit and follows me wholeheartedly, I will bring him into the land he went to, and his descendants will inherit it" (Numbers 14:24). Joshua 14:14 reaffirms that Joshua "followed the LORD, the God of Israel, wholeheartedly." God has a Promised Land for people like Caleb and Joshua whose hearts are full of God and are wholly following Him.

I agree with the apostle Paul who prayed, "I keep asking that the God of our Lord Jesus Christ, the glorious Father, may give you the Spirit of wisdom and revelation, so that you may know him better. I pray also that the eyes of your heart may be enlightened in order that you may know the hope to which he has called you, the riches of his glorious inheritance in the saints, and his incomparably great power for us who believe. That power is like the working of his mighty strength, which he exerted in Christ when he raised him from the dead and seated him at his right hand in the heavenly realms" (Ephesians 1:17-20). You are supposed to be full of it—full of God's wisdom, revelation, hope, riches, and power.

Take Action

- What do you want to agree with God about? Make it something that you have not agreed with God about until today.

- Agree that it's time to agree. Take a moment to recall the last time you had an opportunity to agree with God. If you believe that God's word is true, you can agree with it. What's going to happen the next time life throws you a circumstance? Your response will be determined by whether or not you renew your mind around the truth of God's word between now and then. I want you to go for it! Renew your mind in God's truth so that you can agree with God, be full of Him, and release His presence wherever you go.

- When you mess up and the enemy spins you out, don't let that knock you out for days or weeks. Simply repent, see the situation from God's perspective—He separates your sin as far as the East is from the West (Psalm 103:12)—and get back in the game. That's how we keep moving forward agreeing with God and see the great fruit that comes as a result.

- Pray, *Jesus, I believe in You. I receive You as my Savior and Lord. You're in charge. Give me a heart that agrees with You and no longer sides with the enemy. I agree with Your plan for my life. Forgive me for going my own way and doing my own thing. Fill me, Holy Spirit, with Your power. Guide me and lead me on your narrow path. Help me to cooperate with You and use me to change the world around me. Amen.*

11

Giving Yourself to the Cause

—————

A prophetic act is hearing God's voice and acting on it. Those who love
God will naturally respond to God by giving themselves passionately
to the cause of the kingdom. This produces God's powerful hope in our
lives and in the lives of others around us.

W e're now at the third step to release God's presence
in your life and your city. Remember that all of these
are a package and need to be done together. The progression
goes like this:

Abide: Pursue a relationship like Jesus had with His Father. Stay connected to Him and remain in His presence. His

presence gives us hope that all things are possible with God. You have to see before you can agree.

Agree: See life from God's perspective and get on His side. Renew your mind with God's word so that you can agree with God. Then your soul comes into alignment with the Spirit so you can give yourself to God and do what He says.

Act: Respond to God by giving yourself joyfully to the cause of the kingdom. It's a privilege to share with others what God has given to us as God leads us.

To obey is to give in some way

In the chapter "Prophetic Acts," I talk about the importance of prophetic acts. A prophetic act is *hearing* from God and *acting* on what God has said. Every child of God hears God's voice (John 10:27). God's power comes on the scene when we obey what we hear God say.

I'd like to make our definition of *obedience* synonymous to *giving*. Giving is any way that we offer ourselves to God in obedience to what He says to us.

Giving to Jesus is a light yoke

One of our trips to Mongolia eighteen years ago cost about $80,000. There were twenty-five of us who went. We brought fifty suitcases, seventy pounds each, with six hundred thousand pieces of literature inside worth $20,000. We distributed this "Who is Jesus?" literature all over the country. The Mongolian people had never heard this message before. Some missionaries there said that it was a turning point for the nation.

Even though this mission was expensive, money was not an issue. We didn't have a second thought about this investment into Mongolia. God had spoken to us and we joyfully responded. We had to consider the cost so we could accomplish the mission, but we walked in faith and the provision was there for the work to get done.

Jesus said, "My yoke is easy and my burden is light" (Matthew 11:30). When our giving is simply responding to Jesus, it is easy and light. This is what I call Spirit-led giving. When the Holy Spirit is leading, the amount or sacrifice is not an issue. The issue is accomplishing what God has given you to do.

God wants us to be led by the Holy Spirit as we give. Giving is not burdensome. Giving is joyful!

God is the Source of all resources

I've wondered why Jesus said, "Do not call anyone on earth your father; for One is your Father, He who is in heaven" (Matthew 23:9, NASB). I believe Jesus said this because even though we have earthly fathers who provide for us, our heavenly Father is the true Source of all things. God wants us to look to Him alone for these resources.

At the time this book is being written, the world is in an economic crisis. People are chasing resources, but not necessarily the true Source of all resources. People who have a heart for the things of God will have more than enough to propel them forward. Jesus says to seek Him first and all will be added.

It's easy to see people who are down and out and think that they've done something wrong. The reality is that we can be doing everything right and things get hard. God is setting the stage for many people to be in the same place at the same time so their brokenness brings them into partnership on behalf of the kingdom.

We can learn to give out of a genuine love for God and others. When we see others in need, we can help. If we look to God and are willing to respond as He leads, there's no limit to what God can do in our resources.

There are no unemployed believers

A few years ago I was whining, wondering if I should go back to work because finances seemed to be getting tight. The Lord said to me, "I've given you a job to do. You need to get out and do it." He led me to write a brochure called "God's Real Bailout." He said to me, "Start taking these tracts to businesses to tell them your story about how I bailed you out in time of trouble. I've made you for this time in history."

I met with two pastors in town (Pastor Steve and Pastor Marc) and told them the liquor store story (from chapter 9). I asked them to encourage people unemployed in their congregations to come out with us to pray for businesses. They blessed it, got the word out, and their people have started to come. We've been going out with about ten people once or twice a week.

We've visited six cities so far and have prayed for hundreds of people. We listen to the Lord and do prophetic acts as the Holy Spirit leads us. The Lord shows us to pray over an area, anoint it with oil, and then visit businesses. To cover more ground, we've started to anoint our car tires!

As we seek God first, connecting with His heart for the world, and then build relationships in these businesses, we're seeing God's kingdom advance. Businesses have been very receptive. The first time we visit a business is like plowing up the dirt. When we return to a business a second time, we're welcomed and they're encouraged to see us. The soil is ready and the seed goes in much easier. We're connecting with the people and have heard many testimonies of what happens after we pray for them.

Now other churches in the area are participating. One church with 30 percent of their members un-employed has now asked us to go out with them into their city. People are seeing the value of redeeming the time instead of sitting depressed on the couch because they can't find work. They're working for God blessing people, and they're finding hope for themselves as they release hope to others.

As we've gone out, those unemployed have suddenly received calls to go to work (just like my business suddenly increased when I went to pray for the people who gathered in front of the liquor store). Recently while in the middle of a prayer for a business, one of the guys took a call on his cell phone. After the call he came back to report, "I just got a job and I have to leave right now!" A guy in construction now has more work than he can handle. An out-of-work plumber just got the best plumbing job he's ever had.

We've also been following up with businesses after we visit them. During the week Pastor Scott sends out "My Daily Dose," a daily devotional, to those companies who would like ongoing encouragement (see page 2 for more information).

Across the board, God is providing jobs and better jobs. Those who want work are getting it. Momentum is growing. Many other places are starting to do similar things. Wherever we go, we see God restoring hope and excitement to those getting prayed for *and* those doing the praying. Discouragement is leaving. People are seeing real evidence of God moving in their lives.

God took me off my couch of complaining and others are getting off their couches to get out and encourage others. When people get out and give to the Lord, Matthew 6:33 is in effect and yields great results, for individuals and for the city! The city is reached when we get out and reach people where they work.

Kingdom investments give the greatest returns

The cleanest kingdom giving exchange I have experienced occurred when I was almost out of debt in my business. God spoke to me to give a large donation to K. P. Yohannan (see www.gfa.org). I walked up to him and said, "The Lord told me to give you this money." He reached out and hugged me and said, "Thank you, brother. We really need this right now." Then I said, "Well, wait a second. I don't have the money." He said, "That's OK. If God told you, then let's agree together." We prayed and within three months I was able to write three checks to equal the amount.

More kingdom giving equals more kingdom fruit

I believe that if we did more kingdom giving we'd see more kingdom fruit. There's a big difference between *kingdom giving* and *investing in the world*. I've received the greatest returns from investments into the things the Lord has shown me. I've lost hundreds of thousands of dollars, and friends of mine have lost millions of dollars, on things that *should* work – good investment ideas. God is bringing us back to His economy, His kingdom, because that's where there is the most profitable return.

When you get a little money, you can get a little funny. I got out of debt because I stayed connected to the Source of all resources. I gave what God told me to give. Sometimes that was money; other times it was my time or other resources.

Many times people will obey God to get out of a problem and then stop obeying Him once they're out. You have to know that what got you out of the problem is what is going to keep you out of the problem.

Spirit-led giving equals a great return on investment

The best investments in the world are investing in the kingdom of God. The Bible says, "Whoever sows sparingly will also reap sparingly, and whoever sows generously will also reap generously" (2 Corinthians 9:6). The Bible says when we give all we are supposed to give, God will "open for you the windows of heaven and pour out for you a blessing until it overflows" (Malachi 3:10, NASB). Why wouldn't we want to be a part of that?

The sowing principle applies to every area of our lives. Jesus said that those who sacrifice for God and the gospel will receive 100 times as much *in this life*, plus eternal life in the age to come (Mark 10:29-30).

Many banks are backed by the government so investors have faith they will not lose money if the bank fails. We have something even better and more reliable. Kingdom giving is backed by the word of God and the Creator of the universe.

Everyone needs a home, food, clothes, transportation, and other resources to live. But these things are only *needs* being met. They are not *investments*. When we try to make real estate, a business, or a commodity an investment, and then the market crashes, we lose our investment. When we give the *currency* God has entrusted to us on earth (any *resource* God has given to us and leads us to give), we're transferring it into kingdom currency. Kingdom currency always gets a great return with no loss.

Spirit-led giving is like a great stock tip that guarantees a high rate of return. Excitement and anticipation characterize the transaction. Here's what the Bible promises in 2 Corinthians 9:8-11, emphasis added:

And God is able to make *all* grace abound to you, so that in *all* things at all times, having *all* that you need, you will abound in *every* good work.... Now he who supplies seed to the sower and bread for food will also supply and *increase* your store of seed and will *enlarge* the harvest of your righteousness. You will be made rich in *every* way so that you can be generous on *every* occasion, and through us your generosity will result in thanksgiving to God."

What an awesome return on investment!

Your giving is unique to you

Remember that giving is about how you respond to what God is saying to you. The Holy Spirit will only guide you into all truth (John 16:13). What you give should be based on how God has designed you, not someone else. God designed nature to reproduce after its own kind (Genesis 1). An apple tree does not have to try to grunt out apples. It produces them automatically as it remains rooted in the soil and draws out nutrients from where it's planted.

To produce the kind of fruit that God has designed us to bear, we have to stay connected to our Source. God set it up that way so we would have His life, not just junk food from other sources that only fills the stomach for a short time. God wants to satisfy our deepest hunger with Himself. So we're back at step 1, which is our need to abide in Jesus and stay in His presence.

It's all about Jesus

Recently God asked me, "Do you know what praying without ceasing is? It's talking to Me about everything." If we really want what God wants, there's no other option but to talk with Him about everything.

Walking with God each day is the only way to discover who we are and grow in the way God has designed us. When we remain in Him, we are fruitful as we hear His word, agree, and respond. The same life that raised Jesus from the dead is available to us when we love King Jesus and are about His kingdom business.

Take Action

- I defined giving as *any way that we offer ourselves to God in obedience to what He says to us.* How is God directing you to give today? Consider not only financial giving but also other forms of giving to God and those He loves.

- Dream about how you would like to give if you had the resources? Make this Scripture from 2 Corinthians 9:8-11 a prayer:

  And God is able to make *all* grace abound to you, so that in *all* things at all times, having *all* that you need, you will abound in *every* good work.... Now he who supplies seed to the sower and bread for food will also supply and *increase* your store of seed and will *enlarge* the harvest of your righteousness. You will be made rich in *every* way so that you can be generous on *every* occasion, and through us your generosity will result in thanksgiving to God."

12

No Hell Zone

God is not willing that any should perish. He has
given everyone a key role to make a difference and
release His hopeful presence into the world.

What are you hoping for? A better home, a better job, a happy family? It's OK to hope for these things, but how about hoping for something bigger. How much of God's kingdom do you think God wants to see in your city? All of it! Remember that city I told you about at the beginning of chapter eight? There are cities around the world that are experiencing some of what I described. Your city can be like this city. I can say this because I know how powerful the finished work of Christ is.

Wherever I go, my goal is to make it as difficult as possible for those who are around me to go to hell. Putting into practice what I have shared in this book will help you to create a spiritual climate where people have the best opportunity to come to faith in Christ.

I don't know your specific role in the kingdom of God. I do know it's an important one. Every part of the body is important, and often it's the smallest members who make the biggest difference. Regardless of your role, make a difference and do your part to release God's hopeful presence to those around you.

Begin by repenting of your way of thinking. Enter into God's presence and ask Him to give you a spirit of wisdom and revelation in the knowledge of Jesus Christ (Ephesians 1:17-19). When we change our thinking and agree with God, we activate the power of God in areas that really make a difference in the kingdom of God.

There's always hope

If this book has given you faith, then this faith you've received is evidence that God is at work and is going to come through for you. You may not see it now, but your faith is the tangible substance of what you're hoping for; your faith is the evidence of things you have not yet seen (Hebrews 11:1).

I'll summarize all that I've said in this book with these final words:

- Come out from under the curse and enter into the blessings of God through the finished work of Jesus Christ.
- Bring God's super into your natural by listening to what He says and doing it.
- Persevere and overcome the troubles you face, because sometimes it takes a cloud of dust to make progress for His kingdom.
- Stay in God's presence; keep agreeing with God about what He wants; and keep giving of yourself for the cause of the kingdom.

If you do these things, you'll find yourself full of God, full of His powerful hope, and will see with your own eyes God's kingdom on earth just as it is in heaven.

God has designed you to soar

Let's pray together: *God, have Your way in my life. I want to be full of You. I want to be fully alive in Christ and completely fruitful for Your kingdom. Give me hope for my future and lead me in Your way. Help me to abide in Your love and love others the way You do. Open my eyes to see life the way You do so that I can impart courage and hope to those around me. Show me my role in Your loving family and fill me with Your Spirit so that Your life flows through me wherever I go. I agree with You for Your kingdom to come, Your will to be done in my life and in my city just as it is in heaven. Amen!*

Take Action

- Review the "Take Action" sections at the end of each of the chapters. Renew your commitment and efforts to put into practice what God has spoken to you as you've read this book.

- Go to www.transformourworld.com and join the "Adopt Your Street" movement. You'll find practical ways to reach out to your neighbors and join others in blessing the region in which you live.

Endnotes

1 You can purchase *Thank God It's Monday* at www.rickheeren.org.

2 These steps are taken from Ed Silvoso's books *Prayer Evangelism* and *Anointed For Business*. You can purchase these books at www. harvestevan.org.

www.theprayercompany.com